Happy Birthday

Also by Penny Warner

Healthy Snacks for Kids
Super Toys
Super Snacks for Kids

HAPPY BIRTHDAY PARTIES!

Written and illustrated
by Penny Warner

St. Martin's Press/New York

HAPPY BIRTHDAY PARTIES!

Copyright © 1985 by Penny Warner. All rights reserved. Printed in the United States of America. No part of this book may be used or reproduced in any manner whatsoever without written permission except in the case of brief quotations embodied in critical articles or reviews. For information, address St. Martin's Press, 175 Fifth Avenue, New York, N.Y. 10010.

Library of Congress Cataloging in Publication Data

Warner, Penny.
    Happy birthday parties!

    1. Children's parties.   2. Birthdays.   I. Title.
GV1205.W37   1985   793.2′1   85–11824
ISBN 0–312–36180–7 (pbk.)

Editor: Barbara Anderson
Production Editor: Victor Guerra
Copyeditor: Eva Salmieri
Design by Laura Hough

First Edition
10 9 8 7 6 5 4 3 2 1

A Very, Merry Unbirthday to Tom, Matt, and Becca

Acknowledgments

I want to thank all the party people who shared their birthday memories and ideas or helped in some way to make this book a happy one: Anne Arns; Barbara Bonn; Carolyn, Tim, Timmy, Todd, and Jason Cosetti; Joanne Dahlin; Roseanne and Keri Dickerson; Katie and Jennifer Dubrow; Colleen Dukes; Lucy Galen; Linda Jenkins; Jim Ketsdever; Josephine Kovick; Howard Lachtman; Holly MacLeod; Melissa Maley; Bonnie Matheson; Terry Paetzold; Ed and Connie Pike; Geoffie Pike; Jondrea (J.R.) Rile; Kristin, Brooke, and Sean Saunders; Bill, Julie, Lucy, John, and Joe Simpson; Len, Barbara, Tim, Joe, and Jana Swec; Marion Thatch; Simonie and Mia Thiele; Terry, Mary, and Ralph Warner; Rikki Woodrell; Stefanie van Ogtrop from the Danville Library; Joan Kramer, Ellen Peterson, and the staff of the Nurture Company / Parent-Infant Education; Gary and Christie Nemetz from Cartan's Baby News; Denise Webster from the Red Balloon; Bob Kline, Shirley Davalos, Stephanie Noonan, Jan Rasmussen, Pam Rorke-Levy, Julie Shiels, Miriam Schaffer, and Patrick Van Horn at "T.G.I.4," KRON-TV.

And a very special thanks to my erudite editor, Barbara Anderson, and her meticulous assistant, Stuart Moore.

Contents

Introduction

If you're a typical American family, you have one or more children, each of whom wants a birthday party at least every year until she or he is a teenager.

That means you'll have to organize a dozen or more birthday parties by the time your children are through their teens. And if your children are like mine, they're tired of those impersonal pizza parlor/roller skating parties. They want something *different* this year. Granted, you're getting tired of the large expense those pre-fab parties incur, but you probably don't have a clue how to have a creative home-made birthday party.

Having a happy birthday party for your child will be a piece of cake with the ideas, suggestions, and themes provided in this book. You can choose your own theme by selecting a subject that is of current interest to your child—an event, such as a circus or magic show, that is happening in the community; a movie, such as *Star Wars*, *Annie*, or *Ghostbusters*, that has captured your child's imagination; or a special activity that he or she is involved in, such as playing soccer, reading Hardy Boys mysteries, or memories of the "Pirates of the Caribbean" ride you all took last summer at Disneyland/World. If you're stuck for ideas, *Happy Birthday Parties!* contains twenty-two different themes for parties for children of all ages. Each party idea provides information for personalized invitations, decorations, refreshments, games and activities, and favors. And don't forget that games and decorations and recipes for one party can easily be adapted to other parties throughout the book and, of course, to your own themes and ideas. With a little imagination, birthday possibilities are endless! The parties can be created by all the family members—half the fun!—quickly, easily, and inexpensively.

After deciding on your child's latest passion, you need only incorporate it into these five steps for a successful party:

1. Invitations. Interpret your theme into a unique invitation, using construction paper, blank postcards, smelly stickers, felt-tip pens, and so on, or use one of the ideas listed in the book. You may want to hand-deliver your invitations, mail them, or even make phone calls.

Mailed invitations should go out ten to fourteen days prior to the party and should include the birthday child's name, the exact location of the party, the date of the party, the starting time *and* ending time (parents need to know when to pick up their children), the R.S.V.P. date, and your telephone number. These are the essentials. If your party requires that guests bring or wear special clothes (a bathing suit and towel or a clown costume, for example), make sure to include that information in the invitation. If guests should bring special items (a doll or bicycle or sleeping bag, for instance), include that information, too.

2. Decorations. Using construction paper, balloons, streamers, and crepe paper, you can set the scene and transform a family room into a forest, a patio into a pirate's den, or a garage into a garden. Construction paper is a colorful, economical, and easy way to decorate—just cut and glue it into flowers, rainbows, clouds, balloons, cartoon characters, hearts, gingerbread men, birds, faces, and portraits of the guests. You might also want to attach a variety of store-bought items to the wall—paper dolls, kites, balsawood airplanes, posters, cut-up children's books—which can be sent home with the guests.

3. Refreshments. The cake can be the centerpiece on the table or it can become part of the fun—for example, let each guest decorate his or her own cupcake or slice of cake with tubes of frosting, candy sprinkles, little flowers, miniature toys, miniature marshmallows, chocolate chips, lollipops, paper cut-outs, or nuts. You may want to supplement the refreshments with a few of your favorite treats, too. And don't forget the plates, cups, forks, spoons, and napkins.

4. Games and Activities. You'll need something for the kids to do during the party or your child's guests may become bored and run around out of hand. Party games, appropriate to the children's ages, are always fun but are rarely done these days. The suggestions for games in the following chapters can be adapted to fit your own theme. Make sure to have plenty of inexpensive prizes on hand for the winners! Or you might want to hire a magician or clown, go to a movie or play, rent a film and projector from the library, visit a museum or zoo, go out for hot dogs or hamburgers, try a kid's racecar track or video game parlor, or hire a friend with unique talents—a storyteller, a recreation leader, an artist, a police officer—to lead an activity.

5. Favors. Finally, you will want to send a special "thank you for coming" gift home with each guest. These needn't be expensive if you use your imagination and explore all the aspects of your party's theme.

A few more pointers. Try to keep the party size small. Many people I talked to about this recommended inviting fewer than five children for the two- to five-year-olds, five to ten guests for the elementary-school child, and more as the child grows older. Keep the party short—an hour and a half for the little ones and two hours for older children is plenty. Arrange to have some volunteers to help out—another parent, a neighboring teenager, a big brother or sister. And don't forget the camera (a Polaroid is best) or video recorder—birthday parties make priceless memories.

Remember to understand your child's emotions at this exciting but stressful time. It is not unusual for the birthday girl or boy to spend most of the day in tears or bouncing off the walls. The excessive attention and general stress of the party make many children so emotional that you may want to plan some quiet activities or distractions beforehand to help your child relax. Excessive sweets may also have an effect on your child's behavior, so be sure she or he has a proper meal before the party begins.

Happy Birthday Parties! is a helpful reference you can use over and over throughout the years. The book may also be used to organize monthly parties—for those who just like to celebrate from time to time. With twenty-two ideas for parties, you should have no trouble finding something new for each of your children each year!

Happy Birthday Parties

STORYBOOK PARTY

Select your child's favorite story and build a party around it. I chose the classic *Peter Pan* as an example, but any treasured tale will work when you use your imagination. Each child comes as a character from the book, and games and refreshments are based on the story. And now, matey, it's time ye walked the party plank— aye, it's a pirate's life for me.

Invitations

This invitation doubles as a pirate's toy.

Treasure Map

White construction paper
Black felt-tip pen
Candle and matches
Scotch tape
Chocolate gold coins
1 cardboard tube per person
Gold spray paint

With construction paper and felt-tip pen, draw a map to the party house and mark the site with an "X" or skull and crossbones. Wrinkle the invitation and carefully burn the edges with a lighted candle. Tape a chocolate gold coin at the "X" and roll the paper into a cylinder. Insert into a cardboard tube (you can buy

1

them or use wrapping paper rolls if you have any on hand) spray-painted gold, tape ends securely, and mail to guests. On the invitation, be sure to request that each guest dress as a character from *Peter Pan*, and suggest he or she use the mailing tube as a pirate's telescope.

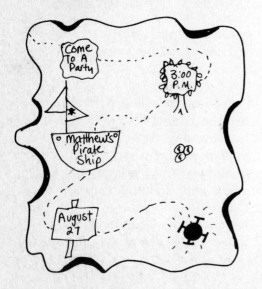

Decorations

Make your pirate's den sparkle with costume jewelry from the second-hand, thrift, and dime stores.

Pirate's Den and Treasure Chest

Construction paper
Felt-tip pens
Scissors
Scotch or masking tape
Peter Pan *Golden Books*
Small, low-sided box (approximately 9" × 12" × 3")
Gold wrapping paper
Costume jewelry
Chocolate gold coins

With construction paper and felt-tip pens, create pirate flags and maps to hang on the walls and to

use as placemats. Cut out pictures from inexpensive *Peter Pan* books and tape to walls and table. Wrap box in gold paper and set on table as treasure-chest centerpiece. Fill with costume jewelry and chocolate doubloons.

Refreshments

An easy-to-make cake—and punch—that'll please Captain Hook himself.

Treasure-Chest Cake and Blood-Red Punch

1 cake mix, any flavor
2 cans chocolate frosting
Chocolate gold coins
Assorted candies
1 12-ounce bottle cranberry juice
1 12-ounce bottle grape juice

Bake a sheet cake, according to package directions, and frost with chocolate frosting. Frost, also, the sheet cake *pan* and set it at right angles to the cake so it looks like an open treasure chest. Decorate cake with chocolate gold coins and as- sorted candies. Serve with Blood- Red Cranberry Punch (mix cran- berry juice with grape juice). Cake serves 8–10. Punch serves 4–6.

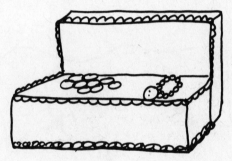

Games and Activities

Have guests dress up as pirates for this part of the party. If they are already in pirate costumes, add ac- cessories.

Dress-Up

Large shirts
Old scarves
Drapery rings (or tagboard)
Scissors
Black felt
Elastic band (or string or yarn)
Brown or black eyebrow pencil

Buy some large colorful shirts from the thrift store and tie the ends around the waist. Make a headwrap using scarves. Attach a drapery ring

Treasure Hunt

Felt-tip pens
Large sheet of white paper
White glue
Chocolate gold coins
Old scarf or handkerchief for blindfold
Stopwatch

Draw a treasure map on the sheet of paper. Mark 5 spots with an "X" and glue a gold coin on each "X". Have each pirate look at the sheet once; then cover the first player's eyes. Set the paper in front of the pirate and, with a felt-tip pen let him or her "trace" a path around the map, blindfolded, looking for the gold treasure. Allow only 30 seconds to find the 5 pieces of gold. Let the player eat what he or she finds. Replace gold coins and turn the map in a different direction for each new pirate.

or ring made from tagboard on one side of the scarf for pirate's earring. Make eye patches by cutting felt to desired size, then cutting a tiny slit in each side. Insert elastic band, string, or yarn through slits and tie to fit at back of child's head. Use eyebrow pencil to draw stubble or mustache on child's face.

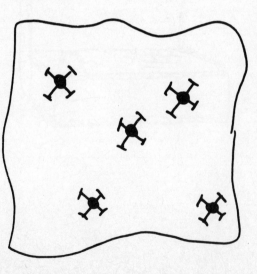

Favors

For favors, you might give out gold gum that comes in a little sack. See if you can find some rubber knives and play money (coins) at the dime store. The eye patches and scarves you made during activity time also make nifty favors. The 45 rpm record, "Pirates of the Caribbean," or a *Peter Pan* Golden Book would be a treasured gift for any seaworthy swab.

DOLL PARTY

Get out your favorite Cabbage Patch doll, Barbie doll, or Care Bear—it's time for a Doll Party! Ask each guest to bring along her favorite doll, and when planning the invitations, decorations, and other details, be sure everything is doll size—remember, they're your child's special guests! Now help your child dress up Tina Patsy or Warren Bailey—it's time for a pint-size doll party!

Invitations

The guests can play with the invitations after they've read the party information.

Paper Dolls

*Several 8¹/₂ × 11-inch sheets
   heavy white paper*
Pencil
Scissors
Felt-tip pens (or crayons)
1 envelope per person

Fold a sheet of paper in half. Using the pattern shown opposite, trace paper doll, being sure that the top of the doll's hair lies on the *fold*. Cut out paper doll through both layers, leaving the layers attached at the fold. Color the front of the invitation to look like a Cabbage Patch or Barbie doll. Open the paper doll and write the party details inside. Request that guests bring their Cabbage Patch, Barbie, or other favorite

doll. Cut out outfit. Slip the paper doll and outfit into an envelope and address it to each guest *and* her doll.

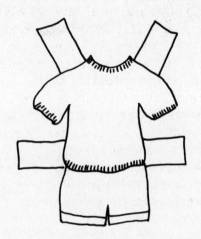

Decorations

In honor of the special guests, make all your decorations in miniature.

Miniatures

Doll furniture and accessories
Thumbtacks
Balloons
String
Doll-themed coloring books
Crayons
Tape or tacks
Large sheets of construction paper
Small plates, cups, and forks

If your daughter has any doll furniture or accessories for her Cabbage Patch or Barbie doll, bring them out and tack them to the walls or set them around the room. Buy small balloons and blow them up only a little. Hang them from the ceiling with short strings or use them as a centerpiece. Buy a couple of doll-type coloring books, then have your child color the pages and tape the pictures to the walls—or mount them on large sheets of construction paper with names underneath to use as placemats. Make a smaller placemat for each doll. Use small plates, cups, and forks for each doll's place setting. As you decorate, remember to keep everything tiny.

Refreshments

Here are two ideas you can use as edible centerpieces!

Cabbage Snatch Ball

Head of cabbage
Toothpicks
Cherry tomatoes
Mushrooms
Bell pepper, cut into strips
Carrot, peeled and cut into sticks
Celery, cut into sticks
Zucchini, sliced into wheels
Any other vegetable you like
Dill, mustard, or avocado dip

Cut the bottom off the cabbage head to make a flat surface. Set cabbage on plate, flat side down. Stick a toothpick into a vegetable and stick other end of pick into cabbage, so that toothpick is hidden. Repeat, using all vegetables, until cabbage head is nearly covered. Let guests snatch vegetables from cabbage ball and dip into dill, mustard, or avocado dip. Serves 8–10.

Doll Cake

1 cake mix
Small round oven-proof bowl
Oil
Cupcake tins
Plate covered with doily

Small Cabbage Patch miniature or other small doll
2 cans white frosting mix, tinted if desired
Decorating tubes

Mix cake according to package directions. Coat small round bowl with oil. Pour in cake mix, ¾ full. Pour remaining batter into cupcake tins. Bake according to directions, allowing a little more time for cake in bowl. (Use clean toothpick to test when cake and cupcakes are done.)

Remove cake from bowl when cool and place flat side on plate covered with doily. Push Cabbage Patch miniature into top of cake, until halfway in. Decorate cake with a layer of frosting, tinted any color you like. With decorating tubes, make stars all over cake and on chest of doll, also with any color you like. This gives the doll a big beautiful dress. Decorate cupcakes—one per guest and one per doll—with leftover frosting. Give the fancy one to the birthday girl. Serves 8–10.

Activities

These activities provide a gift for the guest and a gift for the doll.

Bead Necklace

Several magazines
Scissors
Round toothpicks
White glue or paste
Buttonhole thread (or dental floss)
Large blunt needle

Rip out some colorful pages from your magazines and cut them into long triangles, using the pattern shown on page 10. You should make about 12 triangles per doll. Distribute them among the guests and have them roll the triangles up around a round toothpick, starting at the wide end. Add a dot of glue to the tip and roll it closed. Slip out toothpick. Allow to dry while rolling another. When all 12 "beads" are finished, string them together using thread or dental floss and large blunt needle. Tie ends together and place on doll.

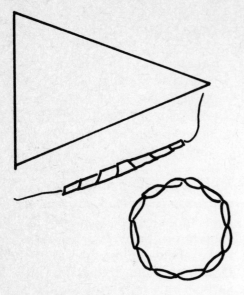

White glue
Felt-tip pens

Take a close-up head shot of each guest as she arrives. Save the photos until activity time. Prepare doll bodies ahead of time by tracing pattern at right onto tagboard. Have guests cut out the heads from their head shots and glue them onto the heads of the tagboard dolls. Have them cut out doll and color in the body with felt-tip pens.

Picture Doll

Polaroid camera and film (or ask each
  guest to bring a photo with a good
  head shot)
Pencil
Tagboard
Scissors

Favors

Your guests will be delighted to take home their look-alike paper dolls and their doll necklaces. You can give them another special gift to take home that won't cost much but will be as individual as each of the Cabbage Patch dolls. Visit your local Goodwill, Salvation Army, or other second-hand store and pick up a few of the smallest baby clothes you can find. If you have a sewing machine, take them in a bit to perfectly fit the Cabbage Patch doll. Wrap them up and put the doll's name on the package. What a delight! And of course you can pick up some Cabbage Patch accessories—little purses, Color-Forms or Rub-Ons, a book, diapers—to send home with the young mommies and their little dolls.

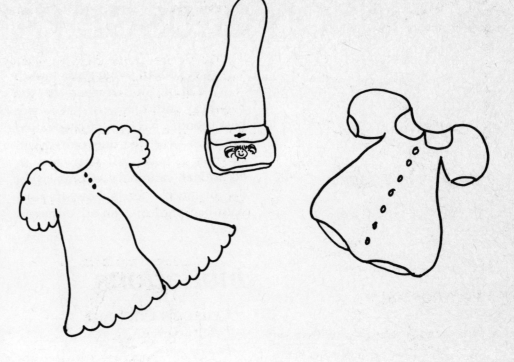

ROBINSON CRUSOE PARTY

Wouldn't your child love to be shipwrecked in the backyard with a few of his or her best friends? No sign of civilization for hours—just the unexplored wilderness, a makeshift tent, and an occasional cannibal's drumbeat in the distance! Here's how to turn your backyard into an adventurer's paradise.

Invitations

Crusoe's Coconut

Felt-tip pens
White construction paper
1 envelope per person

Or:
1 coconut per person
Black magic marker

On white construction paper draw a palm tree similar to the one shown opposite. Fill out party information on the trunk or on the coconuts.

Or better yet, write your information on a real coconut and hand-deliver it to the adventurers. Then ask them to bring the coconuts to the party for an activity.

Since the party is an over-nighter, the invitation should include information about bringing a sleeping bag, pajamas, toothbrush, and flashlight. It might also be fun to have guests bring a stack of their favorite comics to share throughout the evening. And be sure to hold the party on a *Friday* night!

Join Robinson Crusoe at a shipwreck party. Bring your sleeping bag on "Friday." June 23, at 6:00 pm. Don't forget comics!

Decorations

It won't take much to give your yard atmosphere for a Robinson Crusoe party—you have the great outdoors as a natural decoration. But you can add some extra touches.

Tent

You can use a real tent if you have one, but if not, here's a way to make your own.

Piece of rope
Old blanket (or sheet or large sheet of canvas)
Large stones (or hammer and nails)
Tarp

Secure rope to two trees, fences, or other standing structures, about 2–3 feet up from the ground. Hang

blanket over rope and secure corners to the ground with large stones or nail them into the hard dirt. Cover ground with tarp and add sleeping bags!

Forest Eyes

This will be a fun surprise when night falls.

Scissors
Colored construction paper
White construction paper
Glow-in-the-dark paint
Paint brush
Glue

Black felt-tip pen
Stapler (or string or tape)

Cut out some owls or other forest creatures from colored construction paper. Cut out large eyes from white paper. Paint the eyes with glow-in-the-dark paint and glue on black dots in the center for pupils. Staple, tie, or tape them to the trees, fences, bushes, and so on. Nonchalantly shine a bright flashlight over the animals' eyes at dusk. When it's finally dark, the eyes will glow and give the feeling of animals all around.

Refreshments

Stew-in-Bread

Robinson Crusoe didn't have a lot of equipment to help him out on the island. He had to make his own stew pots from French bread, fill them up with stew, and then eat the whole thing! Try it!

Large round loaf of French bread
64-ounce can beef stew or 8 cups of your favorite homemade beef stew
Foil

Cut the top off a round loaf of French bread. Scoop out the bread inside (save it for dipping!) and fill the loaf with beef stew. Wrap in foil and heat in 325° F oven for 1½ hours. Remove from foil and serve on large plate. Let guests serve themselves some stew in individual bowls, then rip apart the "bread bowl" and eat it too! Serves 4–6.

Rafts

Here's a variation on the popular campfire treat, S'mores, so you'll need to build your own campfire in the backyard. (Best place to do that is in a large metal box or pan, or use a barbeque.) This recipe makes one "raft"—you'll need at least one for each guest.

1 skewer
1 marshmallow
1 Hershey-type chocolate bar
2 tablespoons chopped walnuts or
    coconut
2 graham crackers

Make skewers from old coat hangers or other long stick or stiff wire. Skewer marshmallow onto stick and heat over campfire or barbeque until lightly browned. Place chocolate bar and nuts on 1 graham cracker and add hot marshmallow. Top with other graham cracker and sail away on the "raft." Serves 1.

Island Cake

1 cake mix, any flavor
1 can creamy frosting, white
2 cups brown sugar
1 can fluffy frosting, white

Blue food coloring
Small boat and toy tree (or other appropriate small toys)

Mix cake according to package directions and bake in sheet cake pan. When cool, frost top of cake with creamy frosting. Sprinkle brown sugar in a circle in middle of cake. Tint fluffy frosting blue and frost rest of cake, making big "waves" by pulling knife up into peaks. Add small boat to "ocean" and tree to "island." Serves 8–10.

Games and Activities

Here is a whole slew of games to play to pass the night away. The first two are active games to work off excess energy; the last two are quiet games to play in the tent just before lights out.

Save Our Ship

All sit in a circle. The birthday person starts the game by passing a small toy ship (or coconut) around the circle as quickly as possible, before it "sinks." When the parent leader claps hands, the child holding the ship has to reverse directions, again as quickly as possible so the ship doesn't sink. If anyone should drop the ship, she or he is out. The circle gets smaller and the clapping gets more frequent and the ship goes faster and the group gets crazier! Whoever is last, saves the ship!

The Laughing Cannibal

Cannibals are no laughing matter, but this game definitely is. Find a small piece of white scrap fabric—about 5 inches square—that Robinson Crusoe might have used to wave to the ships at sea. The parent leader throws the scrap high into the air—now all must laugh until it hits the ground. When the cloth hits the ground, all faces must lose all expression. If anyone smiles or laughs, he or she goes into the stew pot (he's out). Last one goes free.

Word Chain

The first player says a two-word phrase; for example, word chain. The second person begins his two-word phrase with the last word just

word chain
↓
Chain smoke
↓
smokey bear
↓
bear cub
↓
Cub scout
↓
scout promise
↓
promise me
↓
me .... STUCK!

mentioned; for example, chain smoke. Keep going around the circle until someone gets stuck. Then she or he loses a point and the game begins again with a new two-word phrase.

Predicaments

Even a group of very young children can play this game, as long as they can talk! And the older ones enjoy it, too. Before the party, make up some "What would you do if . . .?" questions. Make them as crazy as you like, but throw in some real ones, too, to keep them thinking.

Here are some examples:

"What would you do *if*

. . . the car stalled in traffic?"
. . . the house caught on fire?"
. . . the house filled up with water?"
. . . the cat ate the dog?"
. . . Mom fell and hurt herself?"
. . . you stepped in quicksand?"
. . . a stranger said 'Hi'?"
. . . your hair fell out?"
. . . your friends told secrets?"
. . . you lived in the zoo?"
. . . you forgot Dad's birthday?"
. . . you were suddenly a giant?"
. . . you tripped in public?"
. . . you forgot your clothes?"
. . . the lights went out?"
. . . a monster attacked you?"
. . . you lost Mom at the store?"
. . . you won a zillion dollars?"
. . . you couldn't find your home?"
. . . your action figures could talk?"

17

Favors

Send the adventurers home with a compass, so at least they know which way to go if they ever get marooned on an island. If you can find some little boats or inexpensive boat models, they make an appropriate thank-you gift. And don't forget those coconuts. If you haven't cracked them open, send them home with the guests, perhaps decorated with felt-tip pens like the one below.

ACAPULCO OLÉ!

Head south of the border for your child's next birthday party with the colors and flavors of Mexico. We've included the traditional piñata, along with some new ideas for party foods, fun, and favors. *Feliz Cumpleaños!*

Invitations

You and the birthday child can make bright, beautiful tissue paper flowers to hand-deliver to the guests; then everyone can make more during the party activity time.

Tissue Flowers

12 8 × 16-inch sheets tissue paper per person in a variety of colors
Scissors
1 12-inch piece string per person
1 12-inch piece floral wire per person
Floral tape
1 3-inch-square sheet yellow construction paper per person
Black felt-tip pen
Skewer or pencil

Layer 12 sheets of colored tissue on top of each other. Cut corners into soft rounds. Accordion-pleat tissue in ½-inch pleats, beginning at the 8-inch side. When pleated, tie off in the middle with string, as shown on page 20. Peel back 6 layers of tissue on one side, one layer at

19

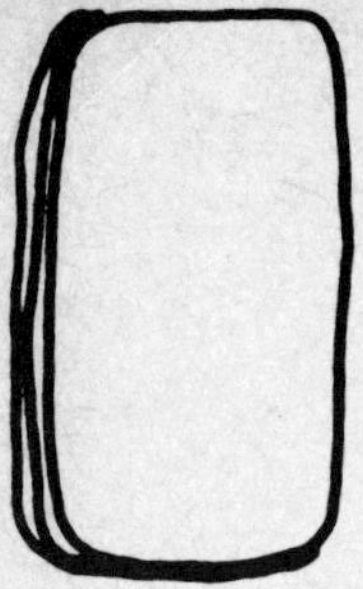

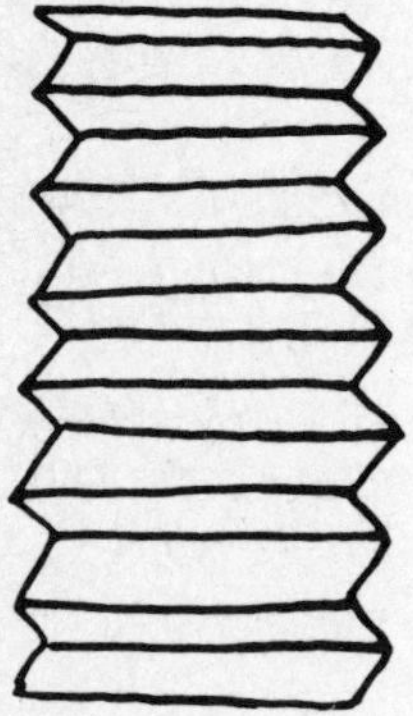

write party information on reverse side.

a time. Repeat on other side. Turn over and repeat twice more, until flower is fluffy and full. Find one string end and attach wire by wrapping floral tape around both, tightly, until wire is completely covered with tape. (The tape is pliable and stretches, so begin on a diagonal and work down around the wire. Press end to secure.) Cut yellow square into bumblebee shape, using the pattern shown above. Add detail with black felt-tip pen. Write party information (in Spanish!) on the tummy of the bee and poke a small hole in bee with skewer or pencil point. Tie to other piece of string. Hand-deliver to guests.

Decorations

If anyone in the family has ever been to Mexico, now's the time to get out all the souvenirs: sombreros, serapes, and papier-mâché bowls and toys. You'll be making a piñata for the activity part of the party (see pages 24–25), so hang it up in the center of the room. Make extra tissue flowers to hang on the walls and windows. Buy a couple of Mexico travel posters to tape to the walls. Perhaps pick up an inexpensive album of Spanish music to play in the background. Make some colorful toucans and parrots from construction paper, using the designs shown. Be sure the birthday child wears colorful clothes, and ask the guests to do the same.

Refreshments

Do-It-Yourself Tacos

Get an assembly line going for Do-It-Yourself Tacos. Prepare everything ahead of time, then line up the ingredients in bowls along the counter or table. Begin with heated shells, then warmed refried beans, cooked hamburger/taco filling, grated cheddar cheese, grated jack cheese, chopped tomato, chopped olives, chopped green chiles, shredded lettuce, sour cream, guacamole, parmesan cheese, and taco salsa. Your guests can pick and choose whichever ingredients they like.

Caramel Lace Pie

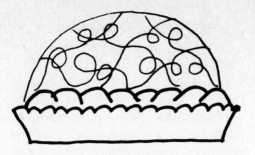

1 graham cracker pie crust
1 quart almond praline ice cream, softened
1 jar caramel sauce
1 quart butter toffee ice cream, softened
Butter
1 large bowl (the diameter of the pie pan)
²/₃ cup sugar
¹/₄ cup water
Whipped Cream

This makes a stunning "how-did-you-do-that?" party dessert.

Prepare or buy graham cracker crust. Spread softened praline ice cream in bottom of pie pan, to half full. Place in freezer. When hard, cover with a layer of caramel sauce and add softened butter toffee ice cream, mounding slightly at the top. Refreeze. Butter the outside bottom of a bowl. Combine sugar and water in heavy saucepan. Cook, stirring constantly, until sugar melts and mixture begins to boil. Continue boiling without stirring until syrup turns a light golden color. Remove from heat; cool slightly.

Drizzle hot syrup from the tip of a spoon to create a swirled, open lace pattern over buttered bowl. Let cool a couple of minutes—just enough to let caramel harden to hold its shape. Carefully loosen caramel lace from bowl. Once loose, keep over bowl to cool.

When ready to serve, remove pie from freezer, add whipped cream to center, and top carefully with caramel lace. Serves 8-10.

Games and Activities

Fiesta Flowers

You can start the activities by having the *niños* make more of the tissue flowers you created as invitations (see pages 19–20). Be sure you have more than enough materials on hand. Then move on to a more active game.

The Cock Fight

1 12-inch strip colored crepe paper per person
Safety pins

This is an exciting Mexican game, named after the popular sport of cockfighting. Have guests stand in a circle and pin a colored strip to each one's back. The birthday person selects two players to stand in the center, face to face, with one arm behind their backs. When the birthday person says go, the two in the middle try to grab each other's strip of crepe paper with the free hand. The two return to the circle and another two are chosen. When all have had a turn, the winners from each couple have another go at it until there is one last winner.

The Rainbow Game

Here's a colorful circle game to go with a colorful country. Have one player select a color. Then each person in the circle says a common phrase that contains the color. If someone can't think of one, she or he is out and the next player tries. If everyone around the circle misses, everyone joins in again and a new color is selected.

Example: The color *blue*

"*Blue* ribbon"
"Once in a *blue* moon"
"*Blue* blood"
"*Blue* lagoon"
"*Blue* suede shoes"
"Code *blue*"
"*Blue* Monday"
"*Blue* streak"
"Turning *blue*"
"Hill Street *Blues*"
"*Blue* grass"
"Man in *blue*"
"Black and *blue*"
"My *blue* Heaven"
"*Blue* collar worker"
"*Blue* pencil"
"*Blue* hills of Kentucky"
"Little Boy *Blue*"
"*Blue* bonnet"
"Wild *blue* yonder"
   Now try *red* ("*Red*-faced"), *yellow* ("*Yellow*-bellied"), *pink* ("In the *pink*"), *green* ("*Green*-eyed monster"), *black* ("It's not all *black* and white"), *white* ("*White* as a ghost"), *purple* ("*Purple* mountains' majesty").

Piñata Pig

You can make your own authentic piñata into any shape you like. Here's how to make a pig. Blow up a large balloon and tie it off. Make a paste of ½ cup flour and ½ cup water and dip strips of newspaper into the paste. Skim off excess with fingers and drape strips over baloon, repeating until entire balloon is covered, except for a small 2-inch-square section. Allow to dry. When dry, pop balloon, cut open a small hole, and fill ball with candy, nuts,

gum, small toys, and other treats. Cover with strips of colorful crepe paper, wrapping around and gluing as you go. Wrap around a second time, overlapping each row and gluing just on top edge. Cut edge with scissors to make fringe. Fringe each row. Add construction paper eyes, mouth, ears, etc. Hang piñata from ceiling.

Blindfold one guest at a time and let each take a turn trying to break open the piñata by swinging a broom handle. *Be very careful* so the other children don't get hurt by the broom handle. When the piñata is broken, let the children go for the candy and treats. Be *sure* to have extra for those children who do not get anything—or encourage sharing.

Favors

Visit a party supply or import store to pick up some small and inexpensive trinkets: little mirrors, God's eyes, papier-mâché animals, little piñatas—anything with a Spanish flavor. If the children made Fiesta Flowers, send each guest home with one. And, of course, send home the goodies from the piñata.

SUPER KIDS PARTY

Is Superman popular around your house? How about Spider-man, Supergirl, or the Dynamic Duo? The Superheroes make great guests at a party, with Super Games, Super Food, and Super Decorations to add a larger-than-life atmosphere. And you won't need Super Strength to carry it off! Holy Birthday Cake, Batman, it's time for a Super Kids Party!

Please come to my Super Kids party for Super fun.

Come Saturday, April 11

2:00

Wear a Super Kids Costume

Invitations

Super Masks

Scissors
White construction paper
Black construction paper
White glue
Skewer
Gummed reinforcement holes
2 10-inch lengths of string per person
1 envelope per person

This is an easy invitation the guests can wear to the party. Cut out mask using the pattern on page 26. Poke holes with a skewer at marks, reinforce with gummed reinforcement holes, and stick a length of string in each hole and tie closed. Decorate one side and write party information on the other side of mask; suggest they wear a Superheroes costume, if you like. Place in envelopes and mail to Super Kids.

Decorations

Spider-man's Web

Straight pins (or tape, staple gun, or tacks)
Black yarn

Greet the Super Kids at the door with Spider-man's Web. Beginning at the top of the front door, pin,

tape, staple, or tack one end of yarn. Pins work best and barely leave a mark on your woodwork.) Begin a "web" pattern, as shown on page 27, pinning, tacking, or taping at each corner. Leave a hole in the middle for guests to climb through.

Super Kids Fortress

Superhero comics
Scissors
Construction paper in assorted colors
White glue
Rubber bats
String
Tacks

Buy some of the latest issues of the Superhero comics and place them on the table. You can also use them to get ideas for decorations. Cut out crystal shapes from green paper to form Kryptonite. Use black paper to make Batman and Robin's masks. Cut out Superman's "S" emblem from red, white, and blue paper and glue together. Cut out spider webs from black paper to make Spider-man's symbol. Buy some rubber bats at the toy or party store. Use string to hang decorations on the wall; hang bats from the ceiling to make Batcave. Make a few extra symbols of the Superheroes from construction paper to use as placemats.

Refreshments

Super Cookie

Toll House cookie recipe (or any favorite cookie recipe)
Large piece of heavy cardboard
Foil
Decorator tubes

This Super Cookie always makes a big impression with the Kids-of-Steel—they can't believe it's a cookie! Using the Toll House cookie recipe (on back of Nestle's Chocolate Chip package) or any other favorite, make up dough. On well-greased, large cookie sheet, shape the entire ball of dough into a huge diamond shape (see opposite). Bake until well-done, about fifteen to twenty minutes—don't take it out too soon. Allow cookie to cool. Gently slip the cookie onto a heavy piece of cardboard covered with foil.

Frost with decorator tubes to resemble birthday child's initial. Don't forget to write "Super Birthday," too. Serves 8–10.

Kryptonite Cake Roll

1 chocolate cake mix
Powdered sugar
1½ cups heavy cream
½ cup powdered sugar
3 drops green food coloring
2 drops peppermint flavoring
1 can chocolate frosting
½ cup coconut, if desired

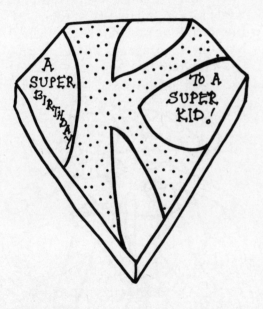

This chocolate cake roll has a delicious green center! Prepare cake according to package directions. Grease a 15"×10"×1" jelly roll pan. Add a sheet of waxed paper and grease it also. Pour in cake batter and bake at 375°F for 12 to 15 minutes (until cake springs back when lightly touched). Turn cake onto clean towel dusted with powdered sugar and roll up cake and towel together at long end. Cool. Make filling from cream, powdered sugar, food coloring, and peppermint flavoring. Beat until stiff. Unroll cake and spread with Kryptonite filling. Reroll. Spread chocolate frosting on outside of cake and sprinkle with coconut, if desired. Serves 8–10.

Games and Activities

Super Body

100 small balloons
2 pairs men's long underwear

This hilarious game will make a Superman out of anyone. Divide the group into two teams and select one person from each team to be the Superheroes—and call them Superman, Supergirl, and so on. Have the two Super Kids put the long johns on over their clothes and divide up the balloons (already blown up for small kids; let the older ones blow up their own). Have a parent recite the following slogan—"Look! Up in the sky! Is it a bird? Is it a plane? No, it's Superman!" When she or he says "Superman," the two teams must stuff as many balloons as possible into the long johns of the Superheroes. There is a 2-minute time limit, so when the parent says "Time's up!", remove the balloons one at a time, counting as you go. Be sure to take a good look at your Superhero when he or she is all "muscles." You might want to have a Polaroid camera on hand.

"Feets" of Strength

Scarf, tie, or small piece of fabric

Divide group into two teams and have them pair up. Beginning with the first two on each team, tie their ankles together as shown using a bow, not a knot. On the count of three, the pairs must race across the yard (or room) and back with their ankles joined. When they reach the group again, they must untie the scarf and tie it around the next pair. If the scarf should come undone while racing, the two must return to the start, retie the scarf securely in a bow, and go again. Whoever finishes the race first, wins.

Favors

Any Superhero comic would be a fun gift for kids. And some Superhero "helpers" for their outfits are always welcome; for example, fake gold bracelets for Wonder Woman, a cape made from red or black plastic (available at the fabric store) for Superman, Supergirl, and Batman, and a rubber spider for Spider-man.

Arms of Steel

Have everyone find a partner. Beginning with one couple, have them sit on the floor back-to-back and link arms at the elbow, as shown above. On the count of three, time them as they simply try to stand up. Repeat until all couples have had a turn. The shortest time wins, and it's fun to watch!

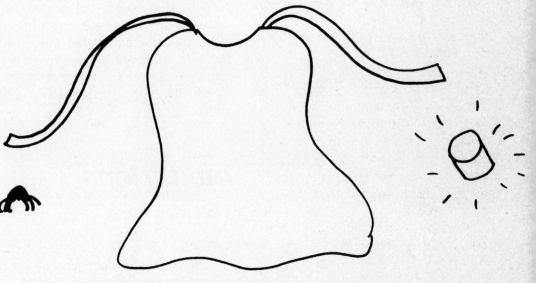

JAWS PARTY

Asummertime swim party is great if you have access to a pool or lake. Most of the time the kids will just want to swim and play in the water. But we've included a few water games for organized play and some alternatives to the swimming pool. So spread on the suntan lotion and grab your towel—the surf is up—but watch out for Jaws!

Invitations

Shark's Teeth

Scissors
1 8½×11-inch sheet blue or gray construction paper per person

Black felt-tip pen
Fine-point felt-tip pen
Glue
1 8½×11-inch sheet white construction paper per four people
1 8½×11-inch sheet red construction paper
1 envelope per person

Cut out blue or gray ovals and fold them in half. Add eyes and nose with black felt-tip pen; with fine-point pen write "Come to a Jaws Party" in small letters along

COME TO A JAWS PARTY

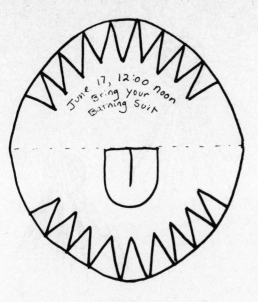

the bottom edge to form the mouth. Open card and glue on white triangles around the edge to form teeth. Glue on a red tongue under fold line, make crease in tongue with black felt-tip pen, and write party information on top. Stick invitations in envelopes and mail to aquanauts.

Decorations

Balloon Jaws

25-30 balloons in a variety of colors
Black permanent felt-tip pen

This makes a colorful welcome to your guests as they arrive at the pool or lake. Blow up balloons and draw Jaws's face on each one with black permanent felt-tip pen, as shown below. Toss into pool or lake (they won't stay around long in the lake but they're not expensive and the effect is worth it).

Super Jaws

Masking tape
Large pieces of cardboard (to equal
* approximately 5 × 10 feet)*
X-acto knife (or strong scissors)
Gray spray paint
Black paint
1/2-inch wide paint brush
6 8 1/2 × 11-inch sheets white con-
* struction paper*
Glue
String

This is impressive when made very large. Tape pieces of cardboard together to form rectangle, approximately 5 × 10 feet. With X-acto knife or scissors, cut cardboard into shark shape, using design shown below. Spray paint one side gray and allow to dry. Add detail with black paint. Cut out triangles from white construction paper and glue around mouth, as shown. Hang on outside wall near pool.

Octopus Centerpiece

3 skeins yarn, all the same color
Scissors
Large Nerf-type ball, 5–6 inches in
    diameter
9 small pieces of yarn (or ribbon)
Glue
1 square black felt

While you watch an old *Jaws* movie on television, wind the skeins of yarn around two chair backs that

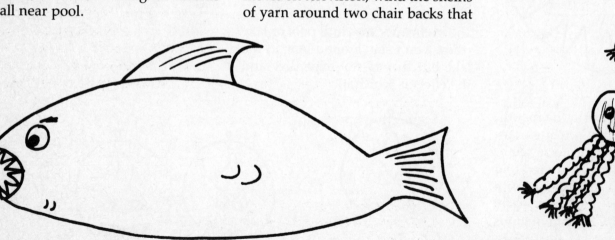

are set about 1 yard apart. When all three skeins have been wound, carefully remove the yarn from the chair and lay it out in a flat rectangle on the floor. Cut through the loops at both ends. Divide the yarn in half and lay the halves crosswise to make an "X" shape. Place ball in the center of the yarn and gather the yarn around the ball so that it is completely covered. Tie the yarn closed at the bottom of the ball tightly with a loose piece of yarn.

Divide the ends of the yarn into eight even sections. Take one section and divide it into thirds for braiding. Braid the yarn and tie off the end with a small piece of ribbon or another piece of yarn. Repeat until you have braided all eight sections. Glue on two felt eyes and a smiling felt mouth. Set on center of table by spreading braids out in equal directions with ball in the middle.

Refreshments

Diver-Down Dip

1/2 pound Gruyere cheese
1/2 pound Emmentaler cheese
1 1/2 tablespoons cornstarch
1 teaspoon dry mustard
1/2 teaspoon garlic salt
Dash pepper
1 12-ounce can beer (the alcohol cooks away)
1 tablespoon lemon juice
1 loaf French bread, cut into cubes
Fondue forks

Keep this pot of Diver-Down Dip heated and ready for a quick snack. Shred the cheeses and mix with cornstarch, mustard, garlic salt, and pepper. Heat beer and lemon juice in a fondue pot over medium heat. When bubbles start to rise, add cheese a spoonful at a time and stir in a figure-eight pattern with a wooden spoon until all cheese is melted and smooth. (If not blending, increase heat. If that fails, mix another teaspoon of cornstarch with 1 teaspoon water and stir in.)

Serve with bread cubes and spear guns (fondue forks). Serves 8–10.

Rocky Road Canoes

1 banana per person
2 tablespoons chocolate chips per person
2 tablespoons miniature marshmallows per person
2 tablespoons finely chopped walnuts per person
2 Popsicle sticks per person
Foil

Here's an unusual way to serve a delicious combination. Peel back one section of banana but don't remove peeling. Scoop out banana, cut into small chunks, and place in bowl. Mix with chocolate chips, marshmallows, and nuts. Fill banana canoe with mixture and cover with peel. Wrap each banana in foil and heat in preheated 350° F oven for 5 minutes. Remove, stick two Popsicle stick "oars" into the sides, place on individual plate, and serve with a spoon. Make 1 canoe for each guest.

Jaws Cake

1 cake mix
1 can white cream frosting
1 cup brown sugar
1 box white fluffy frosting
Blue food coloring
1 package dark-colored fruit leather (such as grape)

Bake a sheet cake according to package directions. When cool, frost with a layer of white cream frosting. Press brown sugar onto sides and up ½" on top to form "sand." Mix fluffy frosting and add blue food coloring. Ice cake top, making ocean waves by pressing a knife against top and pulling up. Cut fruit leather into shark fins. Stick into cake top. Feel free to add a swimmer or two. Serves 8–10.

Games and Activities

Pool Pop

20-30 balloons

Have everyone line up at poolside. At the count of three, guests jump in and try to pop as many balloons as possible using only their hands. Or have them *catch* the balloons instead of popping them.

Keep Jaws Away

Permanent black felt-tip pen
10 white balloons
1 inner tube
Colored balloons (optional)

Divide the group into two teams. Draw a Jaws face on a balloon and toss him into the center of the group in the pool. Have each team try to get Jaws into the inner tube before the other team does by passing him around much like a basketball. If he pops, a new balloon is added and tossed to a member on the other team. Keep track of points. You can make it more confusing by filling the pool with colored balloons.

Volley-Jaws

1 volleyball or badminton net
Permanent black felt-tip pen
1 plastic ball

String the net across the shallow end of the pool and secure it by tying it to a couple of heavy waterproof chair backs. Draw a Jaws face on the ball. Divide the guests into teams and start Volley-Jaws.

Buried Treasure

Pennies and/or nickels

Have guests line up around pool with their backs to the water. Toss in lots of coins. Maybe throw in a quarter or two. On the count of three, have guests dive into the pool and retrieve as many coins as possible. Whoever has the most wins a prize—a piggy bank, perhaps? The rest get to keep the money they found.

Follow the Slider

Large piece of plastic such as a shower curtain (or Slip 'n' Slide or Big Banana)
Garden hose

Set plastic curtain on lawn and turn hose on so water sprays down plastic. Secure ends with smooth

stones if necessary. Line up and follow the leader as he or she performs sliding tricks down the plastic. When all have finished, the next person in line is leader.

Water Balloon Toss

1 balloon for every 2 guests

Fill balloons with water. Line guests up in two rows, facing each other, about 2 feet apart. Give one row the water balloons. When you yell "Toss," the row holding the balloons tosses them to the partners in the opposite row. At that point everyone takes a step backward. When the caller yells "Toss" again, the water balloons are tossed back to row one. Again everyone takes a step backward. This is repeated until all balloons have been *accidentally* popped. Last one gets a prize.

Don't Get Wet

Sprinkler head and hose

Lay hose with sprinkler head out on the lawn. Have guests weave in and out of the sprinkler area. With your back to the kids, turn on the sprinkler intermittently, trying to get someone wet. If a guest is squirted, she or he leaves the game for a few minutes, while you try to get the rest. When all are soaked, play again. A prize goes to the last one to get wet. Make a rule that guests may not spend more than 5 seconds away from the sprinkler—and make them count out loud!

Favors

Send the seafolk home with an inexpensive plastic ball. Visit an import store if you want to give everyone his or her own rubber Jaws as a favor. You might find some seashells and coral there, too. Swim rings are fun to play with, and everyone likes a new squirt gun. Or make up some small-size octopi (see the directions on pages 34–35, but use 2–3-inch rubber balls and just one skein of yarn cut to 1-foot lengths). You can get "Diver-Down" stickers at a scuba divers' shop, too.

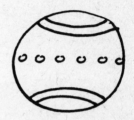

NEW WAVE/PUNK PARTY

Every generation has an off-beat group to parody—does anyone recall the flappers, the fifties, the hippies? This decade it seems to be the punks, a colorful group kids love to imitate. With a little hair color, some clothes from Goodwill or the Salvation army, and the right music, you can turn your party into a New Wave celebration. So mousse the birthday person's hair spikes, turn up the master blaster, and "Let's go crazy!"

Invitations

There are several ways to invite the punks to your party. Don't for-get to tell them to dress for the occasion and to bring their favorite records and tapes.

Records

Scissors
Day-Glo tagboard
Black construction paper
Glue
Felt-tip pen
1 manila envelope per person

Cut out circles in bright colors from Day-Glo tagboard. Cut out smaller circles from black construction paper and glue to center of tagboard circle to form record and label. Write your information around the circle, starting at the center near

Please Please get this party going . . . . some eats and doing some dancing so hurry on over and eats some games, eating some eats and cassettes and show up around 8:00 p.m. We'll be playing albums and cassettes and dress up like a punker. Bring your party on June 23rd and over to my punk.

the black circle and spiraling around toward the outside edge. Place record invitations in large manila envelopes and mail to guests.

Cassettes

If you've got some used cassettes around the house or can get a deal on a package of them, record your party information with some New Wave music in the background. (Or you can buy new blank tapes—but that gets expensive.) Mail the cassettes in padded envelopes. Check the tapes before sending them to make sure the information is audible.

Come to my New Wave Party . . . . . .

Punk Postcards

The record store usually has some small postcards with pictures of the latest musical groups on them. Fill out the party information on the back and stick them in the mail.

Decorations

Most older kids have some posters and album covers they can put on the wall. If not, buy some posters at the discount store and borrow the album covers from a teenager in the neighborhood. If the birthday boy or girl has asked for—and gotten—records and posters as a birthday gift, now's a good time to open them up and hang them on the wall.

Make record placemats from Day-Glo tagboard and use another color as the label. Think of an appropriate song title to write on the label with a guest's name underneath; for example, "Hungry Like the Wolf," by Peter Thatch, "Girls Just Wanna Have Fun," by Lucy Simpson. Set the Album Cake (see page 44) in the center of the table.

Buy crepe paper streamers and hang them about 3 to 4 feet from the ceiling. Attach cardboard 45s inscribed with the latest song titles to the ends of the streamers.

Decorate balloons, using permanent felt-tip pen, with lines from some of the latest songs. Later these can be used in a guessing game.

Birthday girl or boy: Don't forget to dress up yourself. Use mousse to style your hair; then spray your hair with a colored hairspray. With a parent, visit Goodwill or the Salvation Army for your clothes. You might find an old T-shirt you can spray-paint with the names of some punk groups. Or you might find a wild colored vest with dangles. There might be some leather pants or baggy pants—just take in the hem to give them that narrow updated look. Look for wigs, jewelry, earrings, chains, clothes with zippers and rivets—you could even cut off the zippers and rivets and glue them onto another outfit. And buy anything you find in iridescent colors—a definite sign of a New Waver. (Avoid real spikes—too dangerous.) You won't be complete without your makeup. Have a friend or parent "paint" an interesting new look on your face, using colored eye shadows and lipstick, and outlining with eyebrow pencil. And don't forget the camera!

Refreshments

All this music is apt to make a hungry crowd—and we have just the thing to quiet that tummy grumbling.

Skinny Dips

2 potatoes per person
4 tablespoons grated cheddar cheese per person
4 strips cooked bacon per person
4 teaspoons chopped green onion per person
Oil
Ranch dressing or blue cheese

Bake potatoes early in the day for 1 hour at 400°F. Allow to cool, then slice in half, lengthwise. Scoop out most of the potato, leaving about ½ inch rim of potato. (Save potato meat for a mashed potato dinner or potato pancake brunch.) Deep fry skins in hot oil, about 3 to 4 at a time. Drain on paper towel. (You may omit the deep frying and just broil the potato if you like, but this method makes the skin crispy. Or, you can save time by purchasing pre-prepared potato skins at your local delicatessen.) Place skins on cookie sheet and fill each half with 1 teaspoon cheese, 1 crumbled bacon strip, and 1 teaspoon green onion. Broil skins for 2 to 3 minutes until cheese is melted and bubbly. Serve with small dipping bowls of Ranch dressing. Makes 4 for each guest.

Album Cake

1 chocolate cake mix
1 6-ounce package chocolate chips
1 can chocolate frosting mix
3 egg whites
1 cup sugar
¼ teaspoon salt
1 teaspoon vanilla
1 package square-shaped thin mints
Small-holed decorating tube

This is a dramatic-looking cake and a favorite with chocolate lovers. Make a round cake according to package directions, but add the package of chocolate chips to the batter and mix in. When cake is cool, frost with chocolate frosting. Beat egg whites until frothy. Slowly add sugar 2 tablespoons at a time, mixing after each addition. Stir in salt and vanilla. Drop heaping tablespoonfuls on lightly greased cookie sheet and bake at 300°F for 10–12

minutes or until lightly browned. Remove immediately from cookie sheet and let cool. When cool, slice halfway through the meringue cookies with a knife. Using a small-holed decorating tube, write the name of each guest or the names of popular groups on the mints. Insert thin mint into slot in cookie. Place cookies on top of cake in a circle and put one in the middle. Serves 8–10.

Games and Activities

Dance Contest

You can't have a music party without some dancing. This is a good time for the punkers to practice the latest step, make up some new ones, and let loose. But you might organize part of the dancing time into a dance contest, with parents as the judges. Let each guest choose a partner. Tell the dancers they will be judged on enthusiasm, originality, grace, and so on. Begin the music and have the first couple dance for all the others. When all have danced, judge(s) retire to another room to make a decision. *Judge(s):* You may want to have a prize for everyone and present them not only in the category of "Best Dancers" but also in such categories as "Wildest," "Silliest," "Fastest," "Slowest," "Cutest," and so on. In making these decisions, be sure to consider the enthusiasm of the group as each couple danced.

Balloon Tunes

Before the party, write lines from the latest songs on balloons and hang them from the ceiling. At game time, pull down the balloons and have guests sit in a circle with paper and pencil. Pass the balloons around from person to person, each taking a turn to write down the name of the song to match the lyrics. The one with the most correct answers wins. An album or a single record makes a good prize.

Name That Tune

Get out the master blaster (portable am/fm cassette recorder) for this game. The guests should sit in a circle and turn on the radio. Slowly turn the radio dial until you come upon a station that is playing music. It can be *any* kind of music—country, rock, symphonic, Musak—but the first player to name that tune gets a point. If she or he or any other player can also name the performer,

that's another point. (We often give an extra point for a familiar song that has been totally destroyed by an unfamiliar performance—for example, if you hear a rendition of "Thriller" played by Lawrence Welk on his bubble machine, that's definitely worth an extra point. Likewise, the Stray Cats scratching out "When You Wish Upon a Star.") Have a prize for the person with the most points.

Favors

Send each punker home with a top-ten 45 rpm record. While you're at the record store, pick up some Album Gum—bubble gum that comes in tiny album covers. Many record stores also sell overstocked T-shirts for a low price. Or buy posters of the hottest groups, stick them in cardboard tubes, and wrap them up.

STAR INVADERS PARTY

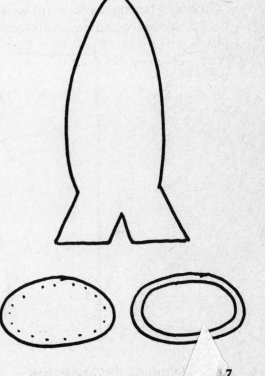

Space never seems to go out of style and if it's a popular subject around your home, why not create a galactic fantasy for your visitors from the outer limits. Fasten your seat belts, Houston, we're about to have lift off!

Invitations

Make the invitations out of gold or silver paper folded into the shape of a space ship, using the pattern at right. Decorate them with stars and insignia, and write the information on the inside of the fold.

Or pick up some inexpensive mini-frisbees at the toy store and write your information on the inside. Then drive birthday child by each guest's home, ring the bell, and let him or her toss the "flying saucer."

It might be fun to find out each guests' birthday and draw a picture on a large tagboard circle of his or her Zodiac sign, using astrological symbols from an encyclopedia or from a library book as guides. Make the invitation in the form of a horoscope: "Your Horoscope for Saturday, May 10: You will be a witty and charming guest at Matt's Birthday Party. You will arrive at 10:00 a.m., wearing a space costume, and will play lots of hyperspace games and eat lots of intergalactic goodies. . . ."

Decorations

There are lots of easy-to-make items you can make to turn your party into the Milky Way.

Silver Stars

Scissors
Tagboard (or cardboard from cereal-
    type boxes)
Glue
Foil
Permanent black felt-tip pen
Glitter
Dark thread
Tape

Cut out stars from tagboard and cover them with foil. Write each guest's name on a star, then dribble some glue on the foil and apply glitter. Punch hole in one tip of each star. Tie different lengths of dark thread to stars and hang them from the ceiling with tape.

Planets

9 Styrofoam or rubber balls in differ-
    ent sizes
Foil
Glue

Permanent felt-tip pens in a variety of
    colors
Dark thread
Tape
Tagboard
Toothpicks

Wrap thread around balls and cover balls with foil. Color the foil with permanent felt-tip pens in a variety of colors. Hang each "planet" by taping end of thread length to the ceiling. Don't forget Saturn's ring (made from tagboard and held in place with toothpicks).

Glow-in-the-Dark Constellations

Glow-in-the-dark paint
Small paint brush
Flashlight

If your party is at night, paint some constellations on the ceiling with glow-in-the-dark paint. (This paint is not visible in the daytime and can literally turn your room into a nighttime galaxy! If you don't like the permanence, paint paper that has been treated with adhesive on one side. Cut out small circles and stick them on the ceiling.) Run a flashlight over the paint just before turning off the lights and you'll feel like you're out under the stars.

Clouds

Polyester fiberfill
White string
Tape

Pull apart fluffy sections of fiberfill to form clouds. Tie white string around two sections and hang them from the ceiling with tape.

Moons, Spaceships, and UFOs

Scissors
Tagboard
Foil
Tape
Mini-frisbees
Dark thread

Cut out moon phase shapes and space ships from tagboard and cover them with foil. Tape to the walls.

Cover mini-frisbees with foil and hang them from the ceiling with dark thread.

Refreshments

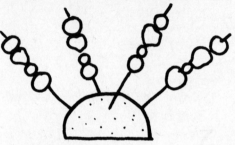

Orbit Fruit

1/2 orange per person
4 cantaloupe balls per person
4 watermelon or other melon balls per person
4 strawberries per person
4 seedless grapes per person
4 small skewers per person
Marshmallow cream

Place orange half on a small paper plate, cut side down. Slide one piece of each fruit on skewer. Repeat with other skewers. Stick skewers into orange half, as shown opposite. Serve with marshmallow cream in small dishes to dip.

Star Cookie Cake

1 cake mix
1 can chocolate frosting
³/₄ cup margarine
1 cup sugar
2 eggs
¹/₂ teaspoon vanilla
2¹/₂ cups flour
1 teaspoon baking powder
1 teaspoon salt
Star-shaped cookie cutter
Colored sugar crystals

Prepare sheet cake according to package directions. When baked and cooled, frost with chocolate frosting. Prepare sugar cookies for cake by mixing margarine, sugar, eggs, and vanilla. Add dry ingredients and chill 1 hour. When chilled, roll dough to ¹/₈-inch thick on lightly floured board. Cut with star cookie cutter into 12 cookies. Place on ungreased cookie sheet and sprinkle lightly with colored sugar cyrstals. Make a slit between two points to center of cookies and spread slightly apart. Bake at 375°F for 6 to 8 minutes or until lightly browned. Remove from cookie sheet to flat surface and allow to cool. When completely cooled, turn two cookies at right angles and insert them at the slit. Place on cake top. Serves 8–10.

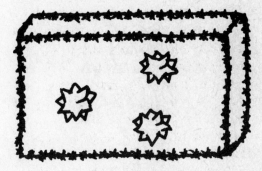

Games and Activities

Costume Contest

Start the activity time off with a costume contest. But why not award each one a prize under several different categories—silliest, cutest, most creative, most bizarre, and so on. Have one grand prize for the best costume, too.

Planetarium

If you have a planetarium nearby, make arrangements to visit it during the party. (You might have the guests change out of their costumes for this or someone may think we have real visitors from outer space!)

Space Sounds

Have everyone sit in a circle. The birthday person begins the Space Sounds game with a noise, any noise at all. The person to the right must repeat the first sound, then add a different sound of her or his own. This continues around the circle until someone forgets a sound and is temporarily disqualified. Whoever outlasts everyone else with sound memory wins the game.

Unidentified Flying Objects

*Helium tank with balloon attachment
(you can rent this for the day)
50 round balloons
50 short lengths of kite string
Permanent felt-tip pens in assorted
colors
Kite string (about 50 feet)
Crepe paper streamers*

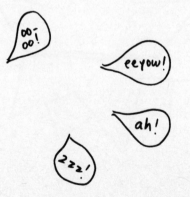

This is a wonderful activity that will fill the time with creativity and fill the sky with color. Have a parent fill one balloon per child with helium. Have another parent tie them off with a short length of string. Let each guest decorate his or her balloon with a strange face, funny message, or wild designs using the felt-tip pens. (Until the ink dries, which takes only a few seconds, it will come off on the hands, so have guests handle it carefully as they color.)

Tie two or three streamers to each balloon string and attach the balloons to the end of a kite string. Repeat the process until all 50 balloons have been attached to the kite string, spacing them out about a foot apart from one another. Take the UFO outside and watch it reach for the sky. With some ceremony, release the UFO into the sky. Listen for news bulletins . . .

Favors

When it's time to beam down,
send the extra-terrestrials back to
Earth with their own model rockets.
You can usually find some space
candy and Orbit gum at the candy
counter to stuff in their pockets.
Pick up some space coloring books
or posters, too.

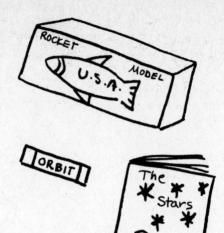

OLYMPIC GAMES PARTY

It doesn't have to be an Olympic year to celebrate an Olympic birthday. If the Games are a favorite with your child, plan a party around the Olympic theme. You can use the same games as in the real Olympics, make up new ones, or try the suggestions here. If the birthday boy or girl is ready to win a gold medal, let the games begin!

Invitations

Gold Medals

Scissors
3 inches each of ¹/₂-inch wide red,
*   white, and blue ribbon per person*

55

1 gold coin candy per person
Fine-point black felt-tip pen
Black ballpoint pen
Glue
1 envelope per person

Cut out ribbon lengths, making a "v" cut at one end. Write "Come to an Olympic Party" on gold coin candy with black felt-tip pen and write party information on ribbons with ballpoint pen (felt pen may bleed on ribbons). Glue straight ends of ribbons to back of gold coin. Place in envelope and mail to contestant, or hand-deliver. (You can also make the medals from gold paper, if you prefer.)

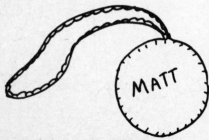

Decorations

Buy some posters of famous athletes and hang them on the walls. Make flags of other nations from white construction paper and crayons and hang on walls (use encyclopedia for resource). Make up gold, silver, and bronze medals from construction paper, write a contestant's name on each one, and use as placemats. Hang Nerf-type and rubber balls from ceiling. If you can find the "Official Music of the Olympics" it would add atmosphere to the party, too. Ask your guests to wear warm-up suits, jogging shorts, T-shirts, and tennis shoes to the party (put this on invitations). Buy some whistles for the referees and have them dress in black and white outfits.

Refreshments

Tater-Toppers

1 large potato per person
1 cup soft butter
3 cups grated American cheese
3 cups sour cream
3 cups chili
1 cup ground beef, cooked in taco seasoning and crumbled
1 cup crumbled cooked bacon
1 cup cubed baked ham
1 cup crumbled tortilla chips
1/2 cup chopped green onions
1/2 cup parmesan cheese

Bake potatoes (1 for each guest) for 1 hour at 400°F just before party begins. Prepare and arrange toppings along counter or table. Place each potato in a small bowl and allow guests to walk around buffet-style and select toppings. Serves 8–10.

butter   cheese   sour cream   chili   green onions

parmesan   tortilla chips   beef   bacon   ham

Gold Medal Pie

3/8 cup corn syrup
3 tablespoons brown sugar
4 tablespoons margarine
3 cups Rice Krispies
Pam (or 1/2 teaspoon oil or margarine)
1/4 cup peanut butter
1/4 cup fudge sauce
1 quart Baskin Robbins Gold Medal ice cream (or any other kind), slightly softened
8 pieces of gold coin candy

Cook 1/4 cup corn syrup, sugar, and margarine over medium heat until boiling. Remove from heat and stir in Rice Krispies. Press into pie or round cake pan coated with Pam or oil or margarine. Mix peanut butter, fudge sauce, and remaining corn syrup and spread half the mixture over crust. Freeze until firm. Spoon in ice cream and smooth top with a knife. Freeze until firm. Just before serving, heat remaining peanut butter/fudge sauce mixture and drizzle over pie. Top with gold coin candy. Serves 8–10.

Games and Activities

Make some gold, silver, and bronze medals from tagboard and ribbon before the party begins.

Obstacle Course

Obstacle items
Stopwatch

Look around the yard and house for about 20 items to use in your obstacle course. Set them up in the yard (or room) for the kids to climb under, over, around, and through. You might try having them crawl under a broom lying across two chairs, crawl under a coffee table, climb over a picnic table, climb through a tight-squeeze cardboard box, walk around a squiggly rope, and so on. Time each contestant while the others watch and see who has the best time. Award the gold, silver, and bronze medals.

Prize Toss

Clothesline
1 clothespin per person
5 tagboard rings, large enough to fit around clothespin
1 small prize per person, each different

Hang clothesline and attach clothespins along the line. Clip a wrapped prize to each clothespin. Have each contestant take turns from the same spot trying to ring a clothespin with a tagboard circle. Whoever makes it wins the prize attached to the clothespin.

Frisbee Golf

Permanent black felt-tip pen
1 frisbee per person
10 sticks, each approximately 1 foot
*   long*

Write each contestant's name on a frisbee. Poke sticks into the dirt at varying distances. Begin at a selected spot and have each contestant, one-by-one, throw his or her frisbee at stick #1. All those who ring the stick get a point. Those who missed must go to the spot where their frisbees landed and try again. Add one point for each throw it takes to ring the stick. When all are finished with stick #1, move on to stick #2. The more points, the less chance of winning! Award the gold, silver, and bronze medals to the three people with the lowest points.

Quicksand Escape

Two half-sheets of newspaper (prefera-
*   bly the sports section!) per person*
10 feet of rope

This is an elimination game to determine the winner. Select half the group to begin and have them line up with their newspapers. Several yards away lay a rope down to designate the finish line. On the count of three, players must try to reach the finish line first, but only by stepping on the newspaper life rafts—

otherwise they'll fall into quicksand. To do this the player must lay down his first newspaper and step on it, then lay the other piece down ahead of him and step on it. At that point he must turn around and grab the piece behind him and pull it around to the front. The two who reach the finish line first will play the two winners of the second group. The final winners receive the gold medals.

Favors

Send them home with all their medals and the personalized fris-bees used in the games. They also might like a referee's whistle and a big poster of a real gold medal winner. Throw in head or arm sweat bands, too.

HAWAIIAN LUAU

There's something very festive about a Hawaiian
Luau, and it's a great theme for a
kid's party. With a little planning
you can turn your family room or
backyard into a tropical paradise.
Aloha!

Invitations

Ribbon Banner

Masking tape
5-foot length of crepe paper streamer
 per person
1 chopstick or pencil per person
Ballpoint pen
1 padded envelope per person

Tape crepe paper streamer to end of chopstick or pencil with masking tape. Carefully write party information along streamer. Roll loosely around stick and place in padded envelope. Mail to guests and ask them to bring along their ribbon banners to the party.

Decorations

Sun, Palm Trees, Surfboards

Scissors
Large sheets of construction paper in
   assorted colors
Scotch tape
White tagboard
Felt-tip pens
Don Ho record

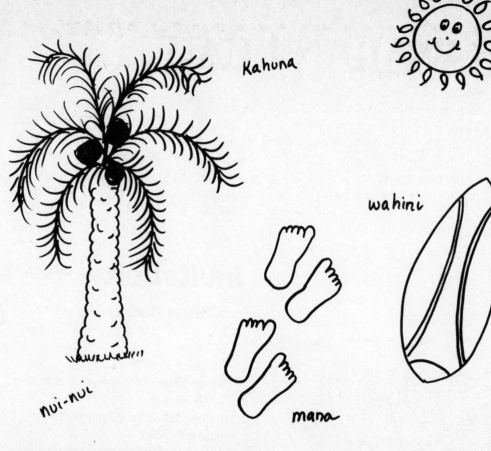

Kahuna

wahini

nui-nui

mana

Cut out a large sun from several sheets of yellow paper and tape on one wall or fence. Cut out palm trees from brown and green paper. Feather the edges of the leaves and tape some of them against the wall. Let other leaves hang out from wall. Cut out a surfboard from tagboard and decorate it with stripes. Set it on the table. Make brown footprint placemats from construction paper. Get a Hawaiian book from the library and give each guest a Hawaiian name. Don't forget to put on the Don Ho record for background music!

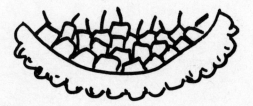

Refreshments

Surf-Capped Pineapple

Fresh pineapple, cut into chunks or
*   wedges*
Marshmallow cream
Toothpicks

Cut pineapple in half, lengthwise, and carve out pineapple, saving outside for bowl. Cut pineapple into chunks or wedges and place back in pineapple halves. Serve with small bowls of marshmallow cream as a dip. Use toothpicks for utensils. Serves 8–10 per pineapple.

Orange Volcanoes

1 orange per person
1 half-gallon orange sherbet
1 tube green decorator frosting

Cut tops off oranges and set aside. Scoop out oranges and fill with orange sherbet. Cap with orange top. Make leaves and stem with green frosting tube and place oranges in freezer until serving time.

Banana Boats

1 banana per person
1 hot dog bun per person
Peanut butter
Raisins and shredded coconut, if
    desired

Place banana in bun and spread on peanut butter. Top with raisins and coconut, if desired.

Cut each hot dog into 4 pieces. Stick all ingredients, alternately, onto individual skewers and roast over barbeque until done.

Give each guest 16 pieces of candy and 16 lengths of ribbon. Have them tie one end of candy to another with ribbon. Curl ends of ribbon with scissors. Connect the last two to form a candy lei.

Games and Activities

Fire Dancers

1 hot dog per person
3 chunks pineappple per person
2 cherry tomatoes per person
1 skewer per person

Candy Leis

16 pieces candy (in wrapper that is
    twisted at each end) per person
16 6-inch lengths of curl-type ribbon
    per person
Scissors

Grass Skirts

1 yard-long sheet crepe paper per
    person
Scissors
Stapler

Your guests can make their own "grass skirts" from crepe paper. Have each guest cut his or her crepe paper into long fringes, leaving about 6 inches at the top for a waistband. Wrap paper around guests' waists and staple closed.

Don Ho Ho

Birthday presents
Hawaiian record, preferably Don Ho

Have the guests sit in a circle and give one of the birthday presents to the birthday person. When the music begins, he or she must pass the gift along to the person on his or her right. The gift must stay in motion until the music stops, then whoever is holding the gift may begin to open it, *until* the music begins again. Then it must be passed on. Continue until the gift is finally opened. Pass it around or hold it up, so everyone can see it, then begin with a new gift.

Sand Pictures

Sand from beach or store
6 food colors
6 plastic containers with tops
Newspaper
Construction paper
White glue

Best to do this one outdoors. Put 1 cup of sand and several drops of 1 color food coloring in a plastic container. Close container and shake until sand is colored. Spread sand on newspaper for a few minutes to dry. Repeat for all 6 colors. Pass out construction paper and glue and let guests draw a design with the glue. Then have them sprinkle sand over glue. Tell them to pour excess sand back into container and then "paint" with another color.

Favors

At the end of the luau, let the guests take home their candy leis, grass skirts, and sand scapes. Import stores are a good source for Hawaiian toys such as inexpensive shell necklaces and other shell items.

SUNRISE PARTY

What better way to start the day than a Sunrise Birthday Party! The dress is casual—pajamas only! Let your guests know something's coming up but keep the exact date a surprise. (Better let their parents know!) So set your clock—it's time for a wake-up call!

Invitations

Sunrise

Create some sunrise invitations like the one shown at right from colored construction paper. On the inside, write the party information, but leave out the date! Mail or hand-deliver. Call the guests' parents to let them know when it will be and ask them to keep it a secret. On the morning of the party, get the birthday child up *early*—6:00 A.M.—and collect the guests from their homes—in their *pajamas!* Ask them to bring a robe and slippers, and

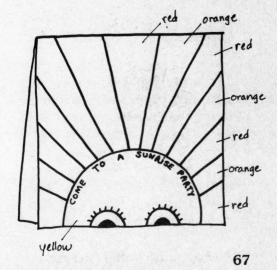

their pillows. Let the guests you've gathered come in with you to wake up the next guest. Serve a small glass of Sunrise Juice (see page 69) on the ride back to the party.

Decorations

Scissors
Colored construction paper
Tape
Glue
1 new toothbrush per person
String

Cut out a big yellow sun from construction paper and tape it to the birthday child's bedroom wall. Add a few clouds on either side and a few distant stars, if you like. Glue paper stars to the handles of some brand-new toothbrushes. Write guests' names on stars and hang them from the ceiling with string.

Refreshments

There are many foods you can serve at a morning party. We've picked a few that are fun as well as tasty and nutritious. If possible, let the guests eat breakfast in bed. Spread a plastic sheet over bed covers and serve breakfast on large plates. Set some small tables around edges of bed to hold drinks.

Sunrise Juice

¾ cup orange juice per person
¼ cup club soda per person
Maraschino cherries

Fill glass with ¾ orange juice and ¼ club soda. Make ice cubes before party by freezing a cherry in each ice cube section. Add to drink. Serve to guests as you pick them up.

Cereal Buffet

Cereal variety packs poured in separate bowls
Fruit (strawberries, cantaloupe, raisins, bananas) cut into slices and placed in separate bowls
Milk

Set cereals and fruit in separate bowls along a buffet counter. Give each guest a bowl and let him or her dip into any of the offerings to create his or her own original cereal—a little Cheerios, a little Shredded Wheat, and maybe some Rice Krispies, mixed with some strawberry slices—yum! Just add milk!

Popover Cocktail

1 tablespoon margarine
3 eggs
⅔ cup milk
⅔ cup flour
1 can (16 ounces) fruit cocktail

Butter a cupcake tin and place in 425°F oven for 5 minutes. Beat eggs, then add milk and flour and beat well. Remove hot tin and pour mixture into cups until about half full. Bake at 400°F for 15 to 20 minutes, until lightly browned and puffy. Remove "popovers" from tins and place each in a separate bowl. Cover with ¼ cup fruit cocktail. Makes 12 popovers.

Cheerios Shredded Wheat Rice Krispies 100% Natural Granola MILK

Strawberries cantaloupe raisins banana grapes

Games and Activities

Shish-Ka-Brunch

2 chunks banana per person
2 chunks apple per person
2 chunks cantaloupe per person
1 brown-and-serve sausage link, cooked and cut into fourths, per person
2 chunks baked ham per person
½ raisin English muffin, cut up, per person
1 skewer per person
1 tablespoon melted butter per person

Prepare ingredients and place in separate bowls. Let each guest skewer food selections. Baste with melted butter and place skewers under broiler for 3 minutes, turn, then broil another 3 minutes.

Lost Slippers

Guests' slippers or socks
Paper and pencil

As the guests arrive, have them remove their slippers or socks and set them aside in a big pile. At game time, line up all the slippers and socks in a row. Give each guest paper and pencil—the goal is to match the slippers to the correct guests. The one with the most right answers wins.

Slipper Scramble

Guests' slippers or socks

Dump all the guests' slippers and socks into a pile, all mixed up. At the count of three, have them race for their right slippers and put them on. Whoever finds and gets them on first, wins.

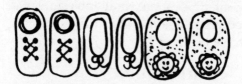

Morning Memory

20 morning-related items (10 nice gifts and 10 funny gifts, such as lipstick, powder puff, pack of tissues, toothbrush, toothpaste, coffee cup, newspaper, and egg timer)
Breakfast or other tray
Cloth

Place all 20 items on a breakfast tray (or other tray). Name each item and tell guests that whoever can name what is missing gets to keep it. Cover tray with a cloth and secretly remove one item. Take cloth away and let them guess what's missing. Whoever guesses correctly first wins the missing item. But she or he must also drop out of the game while the rest of the guests keep on playing. Continue until all items have been won.

Pillow Fight

Pillows from home

Let your guests go outside and have an old-fashioned pillow fight. They probably don't get much chance to do that at home!

Favors

Personalized toothbrushes (use a permanent fine-point felt-tip pen) would be good to send home. Or you can buy packages of decorated pillowcases and send one home with each guest. They might like a perfumed bar of soap or some bubble bath, too.

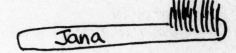

DINOSAUR PARTY

Around the ages of four to seven, most children begin a love affair with dinosaurs. There's something about the monstrous megasaurs that fascinates the young child. Dinosaurs are an ideal theme for a birthday party, so let's head back to the dark ages and see what kind of prehistoric pets we can get to join our party!

Invitations

Dinosaur Egg

Scissors
White construction paper
Felt-tip pen
1 large envelope per person
1 small plastic dinosaur per person

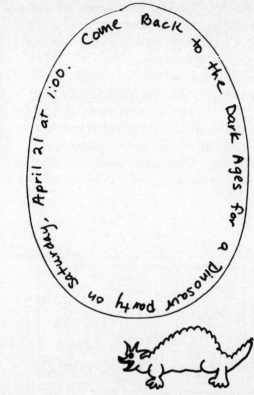

Come Back to the Dark Ages for a Dinosaur party on Saturday, April 21 at 1:00.

Cut out a large egg shape from white construction paper and write your party information on the rim. Stick egg in a large envelope, along with a small plastic dinosaur, and mail to cave people.

Decorations

Creatures and Caves

Set up the room to resemble a prehistoric land by placing a paper tablecloth over a large table or two small tables so that it falls completely to the floor, making a cave. This is where your guests will eat—*under* the table in the cave. Place plastic dinosaurs on top of the table, along with Volcano Cake.

Refreshments

Dinosaur Eggs

12–16 ounces bulk pork sausage
6 hard-boiled eggs, shelled
1/2 cup flour
1 raw egg, beaten
1/2 cup seasoned bread crumbs

Divide sausage into 6 equal parts. Flatten each part in the palm of your hand and completely cover each egg with a piece of sausage. Combine flour, egg, and crumbs. Roll eggs in mixture. Fry in hot oil at 375°F until golden brown. Drain on paper towel and slice in half. Serves 6.

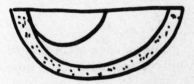

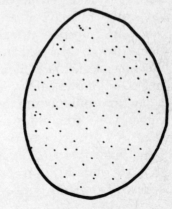

Volcano Cake

1 package chiffon cake mix
1½ cups sugar
¼ cup coffee (beverage)
¼ cup corn syrup
3 teaspoons baking soda
3 cups heavy cream
3 tablespoons sugar
3 teaspoons vanilla

Prepare chiffon cake according to package directions, pour into tube pan, and bake. While cake is cooling, mix sugar, coffee, and corn syrup in saucepan at least 5 inches deep. Bring to a boil and cook to hard crack (310°F). Remove from heat and immediately add baking soda. Stir until mixture thickens and pulls away from sides of pan (but don't ruin the foam by overbeating). Pour foam into ungreased shallow (8″ × 10″) metal pan but do *not* spread. Let stand until cool. Knock

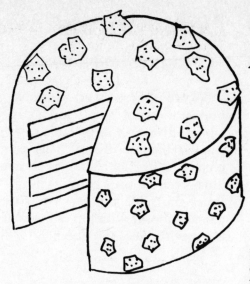

out from pan and break into chunks (to resemble volcanic rock). Split cake into 4 layers. Whip cream with 3 tablespoons sugar and 3 teaspoons vanilla. Spread cream between layers and on top and sides of cake. Cover cake with crushed topping. Refrigerate until party time. Serves 8–10.

Games and Activities

Pterodactyl Eggs

2 eggs per person
Pin
Confetti
White adhesive tape
Felt-tip pens in a variety of colors

Hollow eggs by using a pin to poke a quarter-inch hole in each end, then blowing egg out into bowl. Rinse egg shell and allow to dry. Give egg shells to guests and have them stuff half full with confetti. Tape end closed with white adhesive tape and color eggs with felt-tip pens. Guests then take eggs outdoors and have a dinosaur egg fight by trying to crack eggs over one another's heads. Or have guests sit in a large circle. One player who is It walks around the outside of the circle with his or her egg and finally cracks it over someone's head. The confetti-covered person must run after the egg-cracker and try to get back to the empty spot in the circle before the egg-cracker does. The loser is It for the next round.

Stegosaurus Toss

Paint and brush, crayons, or felt-tip pens
Cardboard box
1 12-inch dowel (¹/₈-inch diameter), cut into 3 pieces
Tape
Bag of curly pretzels

Paint face of stegosaurus on front of box. Poke dowels through to make "horns" and tape on to secure. Set stegosaurus on table and let each guest have a turn at tossing 6 pretzels onto the horns.

Lava Flow

2 large buckets of water
2 empty buckets
1 plastic or paper cup per person

Divide group into two teams and have them stand in line. Place 2 buckets full of water at beginning of

each line and 2 empty buckets at end of each line. Give each guest a cup. On the count of three, have them transfer the water from the full bucket to the empty bucket by passing the water from cup to cup. The winners have the most water in their bucket.

Favors

Send the cavepeople home with a sack of plastic or rubber dinosaurs. You might also find books on dinosaurs they would like or Flintstones coloring books.

CARNIVAL PARTY

You may gear this party to children of any age by varying the degree of difficulty of the games. The skill level will depend upon the developmental level of the group. We have provided a few ideas for game booths here, but the possibilities are limitless. Ask your child to suggest a few—it's surprising what they come up with! And, Mom or Dad, you might dress up as a clown for the event, to add a bit more excitement to an already exciting theme.

Invitations

What a special treat to receive a balloon in the mail—especially one with a party message!

Balloon Blowups

1 balloon per person
Permanent felt-tip pens
1 envelope per person
Balloon stickers, if desired.

Blow up a balloon and write your party instructions in permanent felt-tip pen directly onto the balloon. Deflate balloon and place it in an envelope with instructions to blow up the balloon. Repeat with all balloons. Mail your invitations to the guests. They will have to blow up the balloon to read the invitation. Decorate your envelopes with balloon stickers or drawings.

Decorations

The booths you make from cardboard boxes for the games and activities will certainly give the party a carnival atmosphere. Be sure to decorate them with bright colors of spray paint, crepe paper, felt-tip pen designs, or cut-outs. Here are some other ideas.

Carnival Booths, Clowns, Posers

Crepe paper streamers in a variety of colors
Scotch or masking tape
Posters
Scissors
Construction paper
Balloons
String
Pom-poms
White glue
Colored cotton balls or yarn (if desired)
Felt-tip pens in a variety of colors

Make the room look like a "Big Top" by taping different colors of crepe paper streamers to the center of the ceiling, twisting the streamers as you swag them toward the ends of the room, and taping them securely to the walls or floors. Cover the walls with posters of clowns,

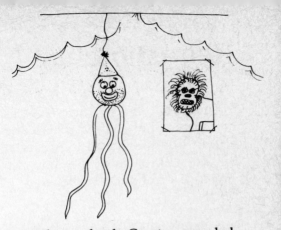

animals, or food. Create some balloon clown-heads to hang from the ceiling: Cut construction paper into triangles and make a cone-shaped hat for each balloon. Tape to the closed end of balloon, running string through end of hat, and top hat with a pom-pom. Glue cotton balls, pom-poms, or yarn around edge of hat. Draw clown face with permanent felt-tip pens, and tape different-colored streamers at the bottom, as shown. Tape string to ceiling. Make as many different clown-heads as you like.

Refreshments

This easy-to-make cake serves as an eye-catching centerpiece, the Clown Cones make nice accents at serving time, and the Licorice Punch is a real thirst quencher.

Carnival Cake

1 package of cake mix, any flavor
2 cans or boxes of frosting, any flavor
2 colors of tube frosting
1/2 cup brown sugar
8 straws
1 aluminum, plastic, or metal pie pan
Plastic animals and clowns

Bake two round cakes from the one cake mix and frost with one can of frosting. Pipe stars around the bottom and top borders with one tube of frosting. Make lines down

sides with the other. Sprinkle brown sugar in the center of the cake to make sawdust and stick straws around the top border. Frost entire bottom of a pie pan with second can of frosting. Set carefully on straws topped with dot of icing for carousel roof. Add plastic animals and clowns. Serves 8–10.

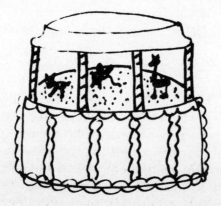

Clown Cone

1 quart light-colored ice cream
1 paper or foil bake cup per person
1 tube frosting
1 can whipped cream
Cone-shaped ice cream cones
1 maraschino cherry per person

Scoop a round dollup of ice cream into each flattened bake cup. Return all to freezer. One at a time, remove from freezer and quickly pipe on collar, eyes, and mouth with frosting; return to freezer immediately. When ice cream is hard, top with ice cream cone and cherry secured with dot of frosting. Serve immediately.

Licorice Punch

1 can (8 ounces) frozen lemonade concentrate
1 can (8 ounces) frozen grape juice concentrate

Games and Activities

You'll need some large cardboard boxes for most of these carnival games. Be sure to decorate them for a festive look.

1 can (8 ounces) frozen orange juice
concentrate
Licorice whips with hollow centers

Mix all concentrates with water, according to directions on cans. Mix juices together and pour into glasses. Cut both ends off licorice and place in glasses. Serve drinks, using licorice whips as straws. Serves 8–10.

Go Fishing

Scissors
Large cardboard box
Large horseshoe magnet
3-foot string
3-foot stick
Prizes
Magnets and glue (or magnetic tape)

Cut an opening in the box as shown. Tie magnet to string and string to stick. Let guests drop "fishing pole" string into booth "pool" to get a prize. Each prize should be wrapped and have a magnet glued onto it so that the pole magnet will attract a prize. (If you don't want to use magnets, have a sister or brother hiding inside the box to tie the string around the presents.)

Nose Toss

Crayons or felt-tip pens in a variety of colors
Large cardboard box
Scissors
Bean bags (squares of red fabric filled with beans and sewn closed or plastic lunch bags filled with beans and secured with rubber bands)
Prizes

Make a large clown face on cardboard box and cut out a large circle in the center for nose as shown. Prepare bean bags and have each guest toss "noses" through hole in clown face. Whoever gets a "nose" in gets a prize.

Jelly Bean Guess

1 large jar
Black permanent felt-tip pen
Jelly beans

Fill jar with jelly beans and set in middle of table with a question mark on top of jar. At the end of the party, have each guest guess how many are inside. Dump the beans and count them. Whoever is closest gets to take them home. (Encourage some sharing.)

Penny Pitch

Large cardboard box
Pie pan
8 pennies or beans
Prizes

Set cardboard box on floor like a table. Place pie pan on top. Each guest gets eight tries to land pennies or beans in pie pan from a distance. Whoever lands the most gets to choose the first prize.

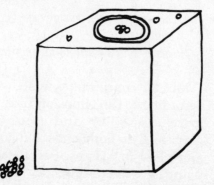

Cotton Candy Toss

Scissors
Large cardboard box
10 cotton balls
Blindfold, if desired

Cut a large opening in a cardboard box, as shown below. Give each guest 10 chances to toss cotton balls into the opening from a short distance away. Try this blindfolded, if the young ones are willing. Whoever gets the most wins a prize.

Mouse Escape

Scissors
Large cardboard box
8 marbles

Cut three doors in box, as shown above. Give each guest eight chances to roll marbles into the box. Whoever is the "high roller" wins a prize.

Ring Toss

Large cardboard box
Glue
6 orange juice cans
Scissors
6 cardboard "rings" (5 inches in diameter with a 4-inch diameter hole in the center)
Prizes

Set cardboard box on floor like a table. Glue orange juice cans to the top of the box, spaced approximately 6 inches apart. Cut out rings. Let guests try to encircle the cans by tossing the rings from a short distance (vary depending on level of children). Whoever gets the most gets to choose the first prize.

Egg Throw

Large cardboard box
Glue
Egg carton
12 Ping-Pong balls

Set cardboard box on floor like a table and glue egg carton on top. Give each guest twelve chances to toss Ping-Pong "eggs" into carton. Whoever gets the most, gets first choice of prizes.

Iceberg Race

Ice cubes
Bowl of warm water
2 chopsticks
Food coloring, if desired
Stopwatch

Drop ice cube into bowl of warm water and have guest try to remove ice cube with chopsticks before it melts. Repeat with each guest. You could make this a relay race and try coloring the ice cubes with food coloring for fun. Award prizes to those who succeed.

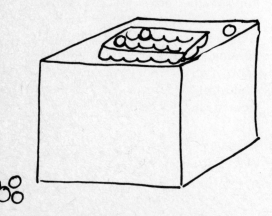

Crystal Ball

1 small piece of paper per person
Pen
1 balloon per person
1 2-yard length of string per person
Large cardboard box

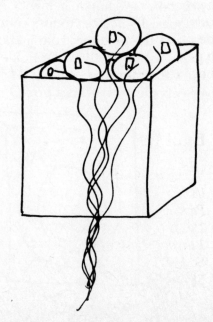

Write funny fortunes on small pieces of paper. Insert fortunes into balloons and blow them up. Attach length of string to each balloon. Repeat until there is one balloon for each guest. Fill large box with balloons. Twist and tangle strings and hang outside the box. Have each guest pull a string and try to locate balloon. When the guest retrieves the attached balloon, he or she has to pop it by sitting or stepping on it, then read the fortune.

Bubbles

¹/₄ cup liquid soap
¹/₄ cup water
Paper cup
1 drop soda pop or sugar
1 drop food coloring
Scissors
Straw

Mix soap with water and pour into cup. Add soda pop or sugar and food coloring. Cut two small slits at one end of a straw and fold back straw along the slit. Dip in bubble solution and blow. Or make blower from stiff wire, bending into a circular shape with a handle.

Face Painting

Moisturizer
Liquid tempera paint, makeup, or
theatrical face paint
Small paint brushes
Small designs to copy

Apply a small amount of moisturizer to child's face—this makes painting and cleaning up easier. Using liquid tempera paint, makeup, or theatrical face paint, transform your guests into clowns, rainbows, stars, hearts, Pac-Men, flowers, and so on.

Favors

The party supply store is a good source for booth prizes. You can buy lots of little goodies for very little money, so that *everyone* can get a prize for *every* game. Suggestions for prizes: clowns, animals, small assorted toys. Or, how about jars of bubbles to take home, the posters on the wall, or the clown balloons hanging from the ceiling?

BARGAIN BIRTHDAY PARTY

A bargain birthday party is a full participation party where the guests go home with nearly as much loot as the birthday person. There'll be some auctioning, some old-fashioned horse trading, and lots of surprises! Going, going, go for it!

Invitations

Auction Chips

Poker chips
Permanent fine-point felt-tip pen
1 padded envelope per person

Count off 10 chips for each guest and write the party information on the chips. Ask guests to bring the chips to the party, along with 3 old toys or household items, wrapped and ready for exchange. Place chips in padded envelope and send to guests.

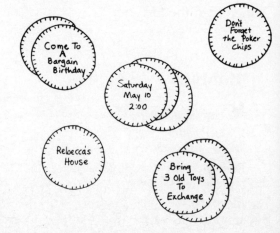

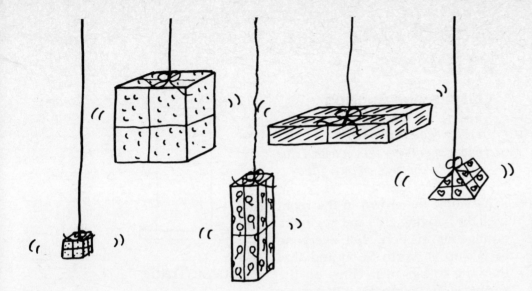

Refreshments

Rocky Road

2 8-ounce milk chocolate bars
1 tablespoon butter
3 cups tiny marshmallows
3/4 cup chopped walnuts

Melt chocolate and butter in saucepan. Remove from heat and cool slightly. Stir in marshmallows and nuts. Spread in buttered 8 × 11-inch pan and chill. Cut into squares. Serves 4.

Decorations

Buy 5 small gifts for each guest. Try to make them all different. They could be anything—comb, hair ribbon, comic book, and so on. Make some of them booby prizes—clothespin, rubber spider, package of paper clips, anything. Wrap them in gift paper and write a clue as to the contents on each gift. Tie a piece of string around each package and hang them from the ceiling. Later they'll be used for a game.

Gift-Wrapped Cake

1 yellow cake mix
1 cup powdered sugar
Skewer
¼ cup lemon juice
1 can lemon frosting
Decorator tubes
Gift tag

Make sheet cake according to package directions. Mix sugar and juice. Poke small holes into cake top with a skewer and pour lemon mixture over warm cake. Frost with lemon frosting. Make wrapping paper and ribbon design with decorator tubes. Put a gift tag on cake. Serves 8–10.

Games and Activities

Outrageous Auction

20 poker chips per person
5 wrapped gifts per person with a clue as to the contents on each gift

Assemble the crowd in the room with the hanging gifts and begin the outrageous auction. Tell everyone each chip is worth $1.00 and that they are to bid their chips on the surprise gifts. Warn them that some of the gifts are booby prizes and that they may buy only five gifts. Pull down one gift and read the clue. Ask who wants to bid $1.00 for the gift. Does anyone want to bid $2.00, and so on. Have them open the gifts as they win them in the auction.

Horse Trade

3 items brought from home by each guest

Have guests sit in a circle with their 3 items in front of them. Let each guest take a turn as horse trader by taking one item from her or his pile and exchanging it with anyone else in the group. The guest must then open the item she or he has received. The next person does the same—*and* he or she may exchange for *any* gift in the circle, even an opened one. This continues around the circle three times until all the items have been opened and exchanged. Maybe they'll wind up with what they want, and maybe they won't!

Favors

They get to take home all the gifts and items they bought in auction or traded. That should be quite a pile!

CARTOON CHARACTERS PARTY

Kids love cartoons. The brightly colored animated figures put children in a fantasy world like no other. Turn your party room into a Saturday morning cartoon backdrop and celebrate your child's birthday with his or her favorite funny friends.

Invitations

Sunday Funnies

Scissors
Sunday funnies
Glue
1 8½ × 11-inch sheet of tagboard per person
Pen
1 8½ × 11-inch envelope per person

Cut out a cartoon strip from the Sunday funnies. Carefully cut away the words in all the speech "balloons." Glue the strip onto the tagboard sheet. Fill in the speech ballons with your party information and mail in a large envelope to your guests. Ask them to come dressed as their favorite cartoon character.

Decorations

Cut out pictures of cartoon characters from coloring books and comic books and glue to your paper tablecloth. Hang comic books on the walls and set one at each place with a guest's name on it. Cut out more

Sunday funnies and eliminate the words in the speech balloons. Fill in with funny sayings about each of the guests. The poster store usually has some posters of the more popular cartoon characters. If you have any cartoon figures, set them around the table. The birthday child might wear the Mickey Mouse T-shirt he or she got from Disneyland. Hang some Disney album jackets on the walls and play Disney music.

Refreshments

Tweety's Fwosty Tweat

1 6-ounce can frozen orange juice concentrate
2½ cups milk

Whirl in blender. Serves 4. Serve in cartoon glasses if you have them.

Cartoon Cherry Cake

1 cartoon cake pan
1 chocolate cake mix
1 can pitted sweet cherries
1 can white or chocolate frosting
Decorator tubes of frosting

You can purchase a cartoon cake pan, like Mickey Mouse or Garfield, at the department or kitchen store and make up a cartoon cake to go

along with your party theme. Mix cake according to package directions. Pour mixture into pan and add 1 can of cherries. Swirl around and bake cake as directed. When cool and turned out, frost with white or chocolate frosting and add cartoon detail with decorator tubes. Serves 8–10.

Games and Activities

Cartoon Categories

1 10-inch square of tagboard
Scissors
Water-based felt-tip pens
Clear Contact paper
Tape
Damp cloths

Make 1 grid per person like the one shown at right, using the same 5 categories on the left but a different cartoon name at the top for each one. Cover the grid with clear Contact paper. At game time, pass out grids and pens to each guest. On the count of three, each person begins to fill in the grid as in the sample. After 5 minutes, stop the game and see who has the most. Wipe off answers with a damp cloth and exchange cards. Try again.

	D	A	F	F	Y
Candy Bars		Almond Joy			
Sports			Fencing		
Slang Words	Darn!	Awesome!	Far out!		Yuck!
School Subjects		Art		French	
Video Games		Asteroid			

Big-Hand Bubble Gum Relay

2 pairs of large work gloves
2 packs of bubble gum (enough for all team players)

It seems like many cartoon characters wear big gloves. This is a game for them. Line up the two teams and give the first two players a pair of gloves and a pack of bubble gum. At the count of three, the first players must put on the gloves, unwrap the gum, stick it in their mouths, pull off the gloves, and pass the gloves and gum pack to the next player. The first team to finish wins.

Who Said That?

Phrases from cartoon characters
Scissors
1 4 × 5-inch tagboard card per cartoon character
Felt-tip pen
Paper and pencils

Sometime before the party, watch the Saturday morning cartoons and write down several characters' identifying phrases. Cut cards into round shapes, like speech balloons. At party time, have guests sit in a circle and pass out paper and pencils. Hold up a character's slogan and let the guests write down who said it. The child with the most right answers wins.

Create-a-Cartoon

Sunday funnies
Comic books
Scissors
White glue
1 8½ × 11-inch sheet of tagboard per person

Place all materials on the table and ask guests to create a new cartoon from the parts of their favorite cartoons. For example, they might cut off Garfield's ears, Mickey's face, and Olive Oyl's body and come up with "Garicky Oyl!" Be sure to have them name their cartoon creatures.

Disney Classic Movie

VCR (rentals are not expensive)
Disney cartoon tape
Popcorn
Felt-tip pens
Lunch bags

Rent a VCR if you don't have one and show a Disney cartoon classic to the group. Don't forget the popcorn—serve it in cartoon-decorated lunch bags.

Favors

Give them comic books—and let them exchange them if they want. You can buy posters or cartoon figures to send home. You can give them the cartoon glasses you served their Tweety's Fwosty Tweat in. They might also enjoy a Disney record or tape.

NURSERY RHYME PARTY

Make your preschool child's favorite nursery rhymes come to life for her or his next birthday party. If you have a book of nursery rhymes around the house, use it as a guide for party ideas or try the suggestions in this chapter. And, Mom, if you can find an old bonnet, a ruffly apron, and some wire-rim glasses, you can host the party as Mother Goose!

Invitations

Hickory Dickory Dock
The party's at 10 o'clock
So dress up nice,
And join us mice,
Until it's 2 o'clock!

Hickory Dickory Clock

Scissors
Tagboard
Felt-tip pens
White paper
Glue
Skewer
Colored yarn
1 envelope per person

Invite your guests with this Hickory Dickory Clock invitation. Cut out a clock, two circles, and two mice from tagboard, using the illustration shown on page 94. Decorate with felt-tip pens. Cut window open at top. Glue a piece of white paper behind it, with party information written inside. With a skewer, punch two holes at the bottom and

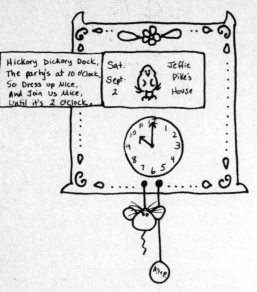

Decorations

Old King Cole
Was a merry old Soul,
And a merry old Soul was he,
He called for his pipe,
And he called for his bowl,
And he called for his fiddlers three.

The Queen of Hearts
She made some tarts,
All on a summer's day;
The Knave of Hearts
He stole the tarts,
And took them clean away.

Make up crowns for the kings and queens who attend your party from gold poster board. Keep them plain and have the guests decorate them during activity time.

Also write nursery rhymes on large poster board and draw pictures to go with them. If you're not artistically inclined, pick up some inexpensive nursery rhyme books at the store and cut out the pages. Glue them onto the posters you have created to add color. Hang on the walls.

run a piece of colored yarn through the holes, as shown. Glue the two mice together, with one end of the yarn in between. Glue the two circles together over the other end of yarn. Write some party information on the circle. Pull the yarn so the mouse "runs" up to the clock. Insert invitations into envelopes and mail to guests.

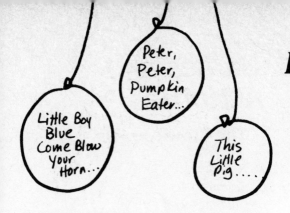

Refreshments

Rub-a-dub-dub,
Three men in a tub,
And who do you think they be?
The butcher, the baker,
The candlestick-maker;
Turn 'em out, knaves all three!

Hang balloons, each marked with a nursery rhyme, from the ceiling. If you can color-coordinate them, do so. For example, Little Boy Blue on a blue balloon; Peter, Peter, Pumpkin Eater on an orange balloon; Little Jack Horner on a purple one; and This Little Pig Went to Market on individual pink balloons.

Make some spider webs from black construction paper by cutting out the design as illustrated at right. Cut out a black spider and let it dangle nearby on black yarn. Write the Miss Muffet rhyme nearby and hang from ceiling.

Three Men in a Tub

1 3-ounce package strawberry fla-
  vored gelatin
1 cup boiling water
1 8-ounce carton plain lowfat yogurt
2 cantaloupes per eight people
3 toothpicks per person
3 strawberries per person

Dissolve gelatin in boiling water. Stir in yogurt and chill until thick but not set. Beat at highest speed until doubled in volume. Cut melons in half and scoop out seeds. Pat dry with paper towel. Scoop whipped mixture into centers of melon and chill until firm. Cut melons in half again. Stick toothpicks in three strawberries and insert into melon "boats."

You can't catch Me—
I'm the Gingerbread Man!

Gingerbread People

1 box Dromedary gingerbread mix
1/3 cup flour
Cookie cutter
Red hots
Silver balls
Chocolate chips
Sprinkles
1 quart ice cream

Before party, mix gingerbread according to package directions, adding 1/3 cup extra flour. Roll out flat to 1/8″ thick and cut out figures with cookie cutter. Wrap with plastic wrap and save until guests arrive. Let each guest decorate one gingerbread person with red hots, silver balls, chocolate chips, and sprinkles. Keep one per person plain.

Bake at 350°F for 8–10 minutes. When cool, spread softened ice cream on plain cookie and top with decorated cookie. Refreeze until all cookies are finished. Makes 12.

Games and Activities

The Crown Jewels

Pencil
Scissors
Gold tagboard
Stapler, glue, and scotch tape
Glitter
Sequins
Gold braid trim
Stick-on circles
Beads
Feathers
Felt-ip pens

Copy crowns from illustration shown on page 98 or design your own, and cut out from gold tagboard. Lay flat and let guests decorate their own with assorted doodads listed above. To assemble crown: Wrap around child's head and mark measurement. Make a cut halfway in on each end on opposite sides as shown. Hook together at slits and crown the royalty.

Humpty Dumpty sat on a wall,
Humpty Dumpty had a great fall;
All the king's horses
And all the king's men
Couldn't put Humpty Dumpty together
    again.

Humpty's Fall

*Large sheet of white paper to make
    brick wall*
Scissors
*Red paint and brush (or red construc-
    tion paper)*

Glue
*Black felt-tip pen (or black paint and
    brush)*
Masking tape
*1 8½ × 11-inch sheet of white paper
    per person*
Double-faced tape, if desired
Scarf or handkerchief for blindfold

Make brick wall by painting large red squares or cutting red squares from construction paper and gluing to large paper. Outline with black felt-tip pen or black paint. Hang on wall. Cut out ovals from 8½×11-inch sheets of paper and draw Humpty's face with felt-tip pen. Blindfold the first guest and hand her or him an "egg" with a piece of masking tape stuck to the top or double-faced tape stuck to the back. Let guest try to put Humpty back on the wall. Blindfold each child in turn for a try.

Rock-a-bye-baby on the tree top,
When the wind blows the cradle will rock,
When the bough breaks the cradle will fall,
And down will come baby, cradle and all.

Rockabye Baby

1 balloon per person
1 12-inch piece of string per person

Tie one end of string to balloon and the other end loosely around ankle of each guest. Have everyone stand in a circle. Recite the poem "Rockabye Baby," and when you get to the word "breaks," everyone scrambles to stamp on someone *else's* balloon while at the same time trying to keep his or her own balloon from breaking. This is a wild one, so you may want to go outside!

Nursery Rhyme Mystery

Book of nursery rhymes
Sheets of white paper
Felt-tip pens

Using a book of nursery rhymes as a guide, draw pictures and symbols of the rhymes on the paper. At game time, hold up the rhymes one at a time and have each guest guess what rhyme it is. See examples below.

Favors

Be sure to send the kings and queens home with their handmade crowns. You can purchase some inexpensive Golden Book nursery rhymes, too. Also, pick up some items that match particular rhymes, such as rubber spiders to scare away Miss Muffet, candles for Jack Be Nimble, a child's dish for Hey Diddle Diddle, and so on.

YOU'RE THE MOMMY/DADDY PARTY

How many times have you caught your daughter experimenting with your blush powder or trying on your newest high-heeled shoes? Have you ever watched your little son grimacing in the bathroom mirror in imitation of his father's morning shave? At your child's next birthday, provide him or her the opportunity to come as Mom or Dad, complete with steam curlers or shaving cream, as the case may be. Borrowing on the "Come-As-You-Are" idea, begin with a surprise invitation, and the "Adults Only" party is in motion.

Invitations

With the "Come-As-You-Are" party, the birthday person calls each of the guests at different times during the day, hoping to catch them in a variety of different outfits. They are to come to the party dressed as they look *right at that moment*. The Mommy/Daddy party is similar, but the birthday person asks what the *parent* is wearing at that moment. The guest then has to wear that outfit to the party. For example, if Mom is getting ready for bed, the child might wear pajamas, robe, slippers, and a wig with curlers attached. If it's cleaning day, she'll dress up in a housecoat and bring along a mop and pan. If Dad is

wearing a business suit the morning of the fateful call, his son can dress up in one of his old ones. Maybe Mom is just getting back from her exercise class—that calls for a leotard and tights. Or, if you prefer to send invitations, ask the guest to wear what the parent wears at, say, a formal dinner party, a cub scout meeting, camping, scrubbing floors, barbecuing, and so on.

Decorations

These two decoration ideas double as party favors.

Photo Placemats

Scissors
Construction paper in a variety of colors

Paper doilies—oval, round, or rectangular
Felt-tip pens
White glue
Polaroid camera and film

Before your guests arrive, prepare placemats from construction paper. Cut one large oval for each guest, an inch wider than the doilies. Glue doilies on top. Color with felt-tip pens, if desired, leaving the center free for snapshot. Write guests' names on individual mats. When your guests arrive, take a Polaroid picture of each one dressed up and glue it to the center of his or her placemat. When the party is over, send the placemats home with the guests.

Parent Portraits

Wide sheets of white butcher paper, the length of tallest guest
Felt-tip pens
Glitter
Sequins
Feathers
Bits of trim
Buttons
Yarn
Ribbon
Tape

Have each "mom" and "dad" lie down on a large sheet of butcher paper. Trace around their bodies with felt-tip pen. Then provide the guests with felt-tip pens, glitter, sequins, feathers, trim, and so on, and let them fill in the pictures as they are dressed. Cut out the finished "parents" and tape them to the walls for the duration of the party. Send them home when the party ends.

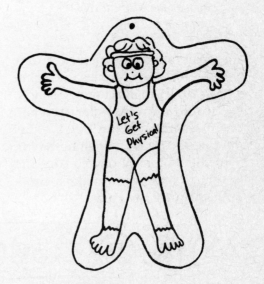

Refreshments

Here's a typical adult "luncheon" altered slightly to please the kids.

Cookie Sandwiches

20 homemade oatmeal cookies
3 flavors of frosting

Prepare oatmeal cookies a day ahead. Shape the cookies into triangles or cut them into triangle shapes when still warm from the oven and save the scraps for the Trail Bar. Let the guests choose a frosting flavor, frost the bottom of one cookie, and stick it to another to make a sandwich. Arrange on a plate.

Chip 'n' Trail Bar

½ cup raisins
½ cup peanuts
½ cup pretzels
½ cup seeds
½ cup banana chips
½ cup granola
½ cup corn chips
½ cup cookie crumbs
½ cup shredded coconut
½ cup carob chips

Place Trail Bar selections in individual bowls and add a spoon to each bowl. Line the bowls along a counter or around a table and let each guest place whatever items he or she desires into one bowl. Designed for eating with fingers. Serves 8–10.

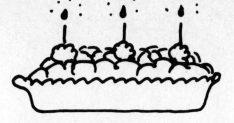

Ice Cream Pie

1 graham cracker crust or chocolate crust
1 quart chocolate chip ice cream (or any other flavor)
1 jar fudge, caramel, or butterscotch topping
1 quart mint chip ice cream (or any other flavor)
1 can whipped cream
Candles

Make or buy crust and fill halfway with 1 flavor of ice cream. (Works better if you allow ice cream to soften for 20 minutes before using.)

raisins   peanuts   pretzels   seeds   banana chips   granola   corn chips   cookie crumbs   coconut   carob chips

Freeze until hard, about 1 hour. Remove from freezer and spread top with a thin layer of topping. Fill the rest of the pie with the second flavor of softened ice cream and freeze again. When ready to serve, top with whipped cream rosettes and insert candles into cream centers. Serves 8–10.

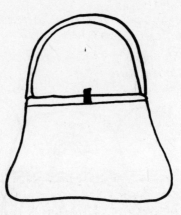

Games and Activities

Here are some games to play in keeping with the Mommy/Daddy theme.

Purse/Briefcase Guess

For purse:
Lipstick
Money
Scarf
Matches
Mirror
Hairbrush
Scissors
Kid's toy
Recipe
Grocery list

For briefcase:
Credit cards
Note paper
Maps
Pens
Handkerchief
Electric Razor
Toothbrush
Memo pad
Comb
Technical book

Fill a purse and/or briefcase with Mom and Dad items and have guests guess what they think is inside. Or, let them see everything, then put the items back inside the purse and/or briefcase and have them recall the items on a piece of paper.

Dress-Up Parade

False eyelashes
False fingernails
Glitter nail polish
Balloon bosoms
Clothing/accessories from thrift store
Costume jewelry
Makeup
Yarn toupees
Sunglasses
Shoes

The dress-up parade is always silly, and you can add a bit more fun to it by providing some extra accents to their haute couture, such as the items listed above. Then take a walk around the neighborhood. And don't forget the video camera. If you have the equipment, show the tape after the parade is over. Or use a Polaroid camera.

Mad Hatter

Felt or Handi-Wipes
Stapler and staples
White glue
Trim
Ribbon
Decals and stickers
Feathers
Sequins
Glitter
Fabric swatches
Rickrack
Pipe cleaners
Pom-poms
Felt-tip pens

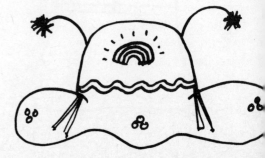

Favors

The placemats, body portraits, and hats should all go home with the children. You could also purchase some inexpensive costume jewelry from Goodwill, the Salvation Army, or the party supply store. The girls might like a tube of nail polish or lip gloss; and all would enjoy a play wallet filled with play money.

There is a popular and inexpensive Golden Book on the market called *I'm My Mommy/I'm My Daddy*, by Daniel Wilcox, that would complement the theme. The mother and daughter (or father and son) switch roles for a day and get a feeling for what it's like to be the other.

Let each guest make a wild hat to add to his or her costume and to take home at the end of the party. Just provide the felt or Handi-Wipes (they're cheaper and work very well) and encourage the children to curve and create them in any way they like. Then add decorations with glue or staples. Allow to dry and then try them on. Have a prize for the craziest one.

Everyone loves a mystery, especially when it becomes a party! Everything is a puzzle—the invitations, the refreshments, the games—with an element of surprise. So don your cloak and get out your magnifying glass—the game's afoot!

Invitations

Stimulate a little curiosity before you invite the guests to the mystery party. Buy invitations or make question mark ones like the model shown on page 107. Fill in all your party information, then cut the invitation in half or thirds. Mail one part to the guests, wait a day, then mail another part, and wait another day before mailing the final part. Better yet, write the information in Braille . . . and don't sent the key until a day later! (Maybe they'll be enterprising enough to figure it out before then!)

A	B	C	D	E	F	G
H	I	J	K	L	M	N
O	P	Q	R	S	T	U
V	W	X	Y	Z		

Decorations

Cut out giant question marks from construction paper and hang them on the walls. Use some for table decorations. Make up some coded messages about each person and write them on a paper tablecloth. Write the decoder on their placemats and let them decipher the messages.

A B C D E F G H I J K L M
N O P Q R S T U V W X Y Z

N O P Q R S T U V W X Y Z
A B C D E F G H I J K L M

Refreshments

The surprise is inside these delicious chocolatey cupcakes.

Mystery Cupcakes

1 8-ounce package cream cheese
$^1/_3$ cup sugar
1 egg
1 6-ounce package chocolate chips
$2^1/_4$ cups flour
$1^1/_2$ cups sugar
$^1/_3$ cup cocoa
$1^1/_2$ teaspoons soda
$^3/_4$ teaspoon salt
$1^1/_2$ cups water
$^2/_3$ cup oil
$1^1/_2$ tablespoons vinegar
$1^1/_2$ teaspoons vanilla
1 can chocolate frosting

Mix cream cheese, sugar, and egg together. Add chocolate chips and set aside. Mix together remaining ingredients (except frosting), beat well, and fill paper bake cups half full. Add a heaping teaspoonful of cheese mixture in the center. Bake at 350° F for 25–30 minutes. Frost when cool. Makes 30 cupcakes.

Games and Activities

Mystery Ride

Load the guests into the van or station wagon and head for a "Mystery Spot" destination. It might be a trip to the movie theater, the skating rink, the pizza parlor, or wherever—just so it's a surprise.

Diamond Mine

20-30 large cardboard boxes
String
8–10 rubber spiders
Tape
Scissors
Polyester fiberfill cobwebs
X-acto knife

This activity is a lot of fun for kids. It's creative and free form and they usually end up designing different mazes themselves. Start collecting cardboard boxes, large enough for a child to crawl or squeeze through and all about the same size. Tie some string around the spiders and hang them from the tops of the boxes inside, and stick on some phony cobwebs. Arrange the boxes in a maze in the backyard, turning the tunnel now and then and creating several tunnels that go off in different directions. Cut out holes on the sides that connect to another box. Let them crawl through one at a time and time them. Then let them have some time just playing.

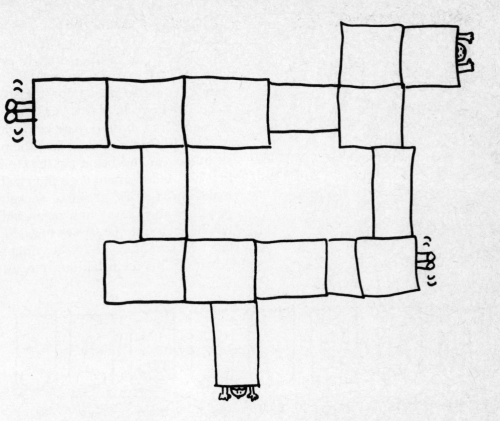

Autopsy

1 old wilted carrot
10 popcorn kernels
½ canned peach
2 large grapes, peeled
1 cup large round noodles
1 cup spaghetti
1 pan of jello (use half the liquid; when set, cut out a 2 × 3-inch oval)
1 large beefsteak tomato, peeled
8 plastic bags
Felt-tip pen

This game is not as gruesome as it sounds, at least not to the kids. They love it! Make up a story to go with the body parts or just tell them they're going to an autopsy. Place the above items in plastic bags, then in numbered brown paper lunch bags, in the order given. Have them sit in a circle and begin passing the first bag, telling them it's a finger. (I make up a story about a wicked person who is sassy to a mean old witch. Each time he sasses her, she takes off part of his body—his finger drops off, his teeth fall out, etc. At the end the witch puts him all back together again.) Tell the guests not to say out loud what they think the body parts are really made from, but at the end let them all guess as you hold up each bag and name the body part. Be prepared—they'll want to do this again and again!

Favors

8–10 very small toys per person
Crepe paper streamers

Wrap up each guest's favors in crepe paper by rolling the paper into a ball and adding the small toys as you go. Let them unwrap their mystery balls at the end of the party.

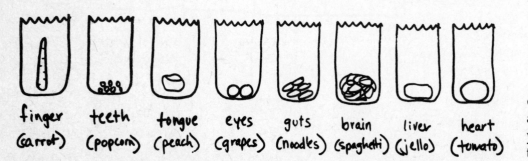

finger (carrot) teeth (popcorn) tongue (peach) eyes (grapes) guts (noodles) brain (spaghetti) liver (jello) heart (tomato)

BEAUTY SALON PARTY

Girls of all ages love to dress up and make up and this is a party just for them. They can use Mom's collection of makeup or buy some inexpensive makeup at the discount stores. Make a visit to the thrift shops before the party day to pick up some costume jewelry, wigs, hats, purses, gloves, and other accessories to enhance the party atmosphere. Here's looking at your kid!

Invitations

Here are a couple of ideas for Beauty Parlor invitations:

The discount stores sell small packages of powder puffs in pastel colors. You could write your party information on the silky side of several puffs with a permanent fine-point felt-tip pen and mail them in a padded envelope.

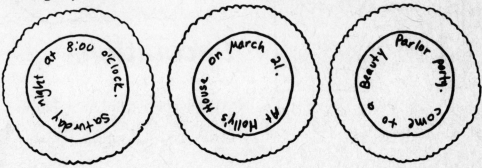

Or pick up some envelopes of bubble bath. Glue a piece of construction paper with your party information on it to the front of the package. Send it in a padded envelope.

Bubble Bath

Come to a
Beauty Parlor
Party
at
Simonie's House
on
February 21

Decorations

Cut out big red lips from construction paper and hang them on the walls. Place a small hand mirror at each place setting and write the guest's name in lipstick on the mirror. Hang combs from the ceiling with string and lay *Glamour*, *Seventeen*, and *Mademoiselle* on the table.

Refreshments

Devil's Fingers

1 cup deviled ham
1 cup deviled egg
Mayonnaise
Mustard
8 slices tinted bread (available from the bakery by request—choose your favorite colors)

Prepare the deviled ham and egg mix by combining with a little mayonnaise and mustard. Cut crust off bread and spread mixture on slices. Top with another slice and cut sandwiches into rectangular fingers. Serves 4.

Cream Puffs

¹/₂ cup butter
1 cup water
1 cup flour
¹/₄ teaspoon salt
4 eggs
1 8-ounce package vanilla or lemon pudding
1 can chocolate frosting
3 tablespoons water
1 maraschino cherry per person

Place butter and water in saucepan and bring to a boil. Add flour and salt and mix well. Cook until mixture pulls away from the sides of the pan. Remove from heat. Beat eggs and add to mixture. Beat well. Drop tablespoonfuls onto greased cookie sheet, 2 inches apart, and bake at 450° F for 15 minutes. Reduce heat to 325° F and bake 20 more minutes. Make pudding according to package directions and cool in refrigerator. When set, slit puffs and fill with 2 heaping tablespoons pudding. Scoop frosting into bowl and add water. Stir with a spoon until frosting is thinned. Add more water if necessary. Frost top of cream puffs and add a cherry to the top. Makes 8–10 cream puffs.

Games and Activities

Dress-Up/Make-Up

Lipsticks
Lip brush
Nail polishes

Fake eyelashes and glue
Nail decals
Fake nails
Blushers
Brushes
Powders
Powder puffs
Eyebrow pencils
Eye shadows
Face glitter
Clown white
Jewelry, wigs, hats, and so on

The guests will probably spend a good portion of this party just making up. Have a contest for the most beautiful, the most bizarre, the most New Wave, the funniest, and so on. Pick out bright lipsticks and some in unusual colors and let them try their hands at a lip brush. Pick out nail polish in bright colors and some with glitter. Provide decals for the nails and some phony fingernails, too. Buy a couple of pairs of fake eyelashes and glue and have the guests take turns with them. Set out blushers and brushes, powders and puffs for the face. Let them design new faces with eyebrow pencils. Fill in with colored eye shadow, face glitter, and clown white. Add jewelry, wigs, etc.

Broken Mirror

Give each person a turn at the Broken Mirror game. Set out 1 lipstick, 1 blush color, 1 eye shadow, 1 eyebrow pencil, and 1 mascara. Tell the first guest she has 30 seconds to get her makeup on and has just broken her mirror. Let each person have a try. See who does the best job, the worst job, for prizes. (Wipe off lipstick with a tissue for each guest's use.)

Dangle Barrettes

2 lengths of 1¼ yards ribbon (⅛ inch wide) in 2 different colors per person
1 plain barrette with slit down the middle, as shown below, per person
Scissors
1 small heart button (or other button) per person
Tiny artificial flowers, if desired
2 small beads per person, if desired

Have each guest tie one end of each ribbon together so that she has one long piece. Beginning at the open end of the barrette, insert one end of ribbon through the slit and pull through, then do the same with the other color on the other side, repeating this weaving motion until barrette is completely woven. Tie off and let ribbon ends dangle down; cut ends at angle. Sew on cute heart or other button, or glue on tiny artificial flowers at closed end of barrette to hide knot. Tie small bead to dangle ends, if desired.

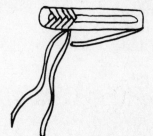

Lace Barrettes

Needles and thread
1 small plastic clip-on barrette per person
¼ yard eyelet lace (³/4 inch wide) per person
2 strips of ribbon (each ¼ yard long and ¼ inch wide) per person
1 cute little button per person

Have each guest sew along plain edge of lace lengthwise and gather up. Form into a silver dollar-size circle and stitch edges together. Sew onto open barrette, looping around to secure it and leaving clip part free. Tie two colors of ribbon into a small bow, so that ribbon has a two-toned look. Center on lace and stitch. Center a cute button on bow and sew on.

Favors

Send home the barrettes they made (or you can make them for the guests ahead of time). Give them a selection of makeup—polish, lipstick, phony nails—and let them have the little hand mirrors to take home, too.

HOLLYWOOD PARTY

Lights! Camera! It's time for a Hollywood Party. Here's a chance for your child to become one of his or her favorite characters of stage, screen, or boob tube and celebrate a birthday among the celebrities. You never know who might show up—Dolly Parton, Superman, Frankenstein, even Benji! Let's roll those cameras. It's time for some *action!*

Invitations

Here are a couple of suggestions for Hollywood invitations.

Admission Tickets

Gold paper
Scissors
Fine-point permanent black felt-tip pen
1 envelope per person
Gummed stars

Cut gold paper into 2×3-inch rectangles. Cut edges in scallops at both ends. Copy ticket format shown at left with felt-tip pen, filling in your party details. Place in

Come to my Hollywood party
ADMIT ONE
Saturday 3:00 P.M. APRIL 21

envelopes decorated with gummed stars, and mail to guests.

Rising Star Cookie Pops

4 cups flour
½ cup honey
1 cup butter
1 beaten egg
Star-shaped cookie cutter
6 Popsicle sticks
Several tubes different colored frosting
Felt-tip pens
6 3-inch-square cards
6 foot-long pieces yarn

Mix flour, honey, butter, and egg together and chill dough. When firm, roll to ½ inch thick and cut into stars. Place on well-greased cookie sheet and bake 6–8 minutes at 350° F. Insert Popsicle sticks into cookies while still warm. Decorate

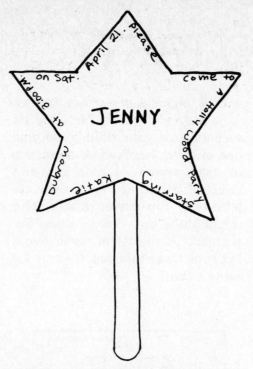

with frosting and add party details or fill out party information on small cards and attach to sticks with yarn. Carefully hand-deliver to rising young stars. Makes 6 invitations.

Decorations

Stars

Star-shaped cookie cutter
Construction paper in assorted colors
Scissors
Black felt-tip pen
Scotch tape

Dazzle your child's friends with stars. Using a cookie cutter as a guide, cut out lots of stars from construction paper. Write the names of the kids' favorite stars inside. Make up some with the guests' names, too. You can use these later for a game. Tape them all over the party area and front door.

Stiffs

Large panels of cardboard (they may
  be taped together)
Posters of favorite stars
Scissors
White glue
Black or white paint
Paint brush

Stiffs make quite an impression on your guests as they arrive because they can look so real! Collect large cardboard pieces or tape smaller pieces together to form panels approximately 3 × 4 feet. Buy as many posters of your child's favorite stars as you can afford. Cut out the stars and glue them to the cardboard panels. Cut out the cardboard panels along the poster edge. Paint the backsides white or black and stick a large star in the middle of the back. Set your stiffs at each place at the table so that it looks like Brooke Shields, Matt Dillon, and Bugs Bunny are your guests, too.

MATT DILLON

Rainbow Brite

BROOKE SHIELDS

Refreshments

Starwich

1 loaf each of bread tinted pink, yellow, and blue (order from a bakery)
1 jar peanut butter
1 jar jelly
1 bag corn chips

Buy tinted bread from the bakery and have them slice it into thin sandwich slices. Trim off crust and make up peanut butter and jelly sandwiches. Cut into triangles and place five alternating colors in paper plate to form a star. Fill center with corn chips.

Shirley Temple and Roy Rogers

1 32-ounce bottle ginger ale
1 32-ounce bottle cola
1 small bottle cherry juice
1 maraschino cherry per person

Ask guests which drink they prefer—Shirley Temple (made with ginger ale) or Roy Rogers (made with cola). Fill glasses nearly full with ale or cola, then add 1 tablespoon cherry juice and a cherry.

Handprint Star Cake

1 package cake mix
1 can light-colored frosting
Decorator tubes in red, blue, and green

To make your own "Handprints of the Stars" like they do at Grauman's Chinese Theatre, first prepare cake according to package directions. Pour batter equally into rectangular cake pan and round cake pan. When cool, cut rectangular cake as shown opposite, and set tips around round cake to form star. Cover with frosting as shown. Trace

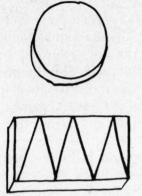

hand of birthday person on a piece of paper. Cut out and lightly lay paper in center of cake. With a toothpick, outline hand by poking tiny holes around edge. Remove paper and outline with decorator tube. Write "Happy Birthday" and name of birthday star on either side of handprint. Serves 8–10.

Games and Activities

There are lots of games for the Hollywood crowd so let's get started.

Return of the Mummy

2 rolls toilet paper

Here's a game from one of Hollywood's best monster films, *The Mummy's Curse*. Divide guests into two teams. Choose two people to be mummies, one from each team. On the count of three, the first teammate begins to wrap the mummy. If the toilet paper breaks, the roll is passed on to the second teammate, who continues from where the other left off, until the mummy is completely wrapped up—except for eyes, nose, and mouth. It breaks easily, especially when you're in a hurry, so everyone should get a turn.

Famous Faces

Scissors
Teen or movie magazines with lots of large pictures of popular stars
Glue
Ruler
Tagboard
Black felt-tip pen
Large manila envelopes

Cut out pictures of movie stars and glue them onto tagboard. Mark off ½-inch spaces on either side of

the photo, then draw lines connecting the marks so that you have black lines running down the page at ½-inch intervals. Slip the photo, head up, into a manila envelope. Make several of these. At game time, have everyone sit facing the birthday child. He or she opens the first envelope and pulls the photo out to the first black line. Can anyone guess who it is? No? Move to the next black line. Have them continue to guess until someone finally recognizes each face.

Name Dropper

Construction paper stars
Black felt-tip pen
Safety pins

Think up some popular movie stars and write their names on the construction paper stars. Pin them on your guests as they arrive and tell them not to tell anyone the name of the star on anyone else's back. When all have arrived, have them try to guess who they are, by asking questions about them. Here are some good questions to ask:
"Am I a male (or female)?"
"Am I a child (or an adult)?"
"Am I real (or fictional)?"
"Do I sing (or dance)?"
"Am I on T.V. (or in the movies)?"
And so on.

Cryptic Characters

Posterboard
Felt-tip pen
Pencils and paper
Tape

Write a list of "Characters" on one side of a posterboard and a list of "Movie Titles" on the back (see sample on page 124). Tape the board on a wall. Distribute paper and pencils and have guests write down the names of the characters that are listed on your chart. Of course, you've forgotten to include the vowels so it might be a bit tricky. . . . (Tell them to try sounding the words out and that will help.) After a set time limit, find out who has deciphered the most characters. Then turn the board over and play the game with movie titles. If you don't want to use the list below, you can make up your own.

Characters
GRCLMN (Gary Coleman)
PPY (Popeye)
MRK (Mork)
WDWDPCKR (Woody Woodpecker)
PCMN (Pac-man)
GRGML (Gargamel)
SPRMN (Superman)
TMSWYR (Tom Sawyer)
NNCDRW (Nancy Drew)
CSPR (Casper)

Movie Titles
NN (Annie)
T (E.T.)
BBTTNDCSTLLMTFRNKNSTN (Abbot and Costello Meet Frankenstein)
DRKCRSTL (Dark Crystal)
GHSTBSTRS (Ghostbusters)
RSCRS (Rescuers)
BMB (Bambi)
RPLN (Airplane)
JWS (Jaws)
SNWWHTNDTHSVNDWRFS (Snow White and the Seven Dwarfs)

Screen Test

VCR
Videotape
Popcorn

If you don't own one, you can rent a videocassette recorder for a very low price today. Tape your guests as they arrive, as they play games, as they eat refreshments. Then at the end of the party, show the "movie." Don't forget the popcorn!

Favors

Sardi's Stars

4 cups flour
1 cup salt
1¾ cups water

Food coloring
Star-shaped cookie cutter
Knife
Paper clips
Shellac
Brush
Polaroid camera and film
Glue

Before the party, make up some Baker's Clay, using the flour, salt, and water. Divide the dough into 4 balls and color each with a different shade of food coloring. Roll dough out to ¼-inch thick and cut out stars. With a knife, cut out center following star shape. Insert a paper clip in one point, about halfway in, to form hook for hanging. Bake stars at 250°F for 2–3 hours, until hard. Coat with shellac and let dry. Take pictures of guests as they arrive and, using star-shaped cookie cutter, cut out photos. Glue to back of dough so picture is framed by star. Hang at Sardi's or hand to guests as they leave. Makes 8–10 stars.

You can also add to the fun by giving the stars sunglasses, teen movie magazines, and posters of some of the popular stars.

'ROUND THE WORLD PARTY

Take the best birthday ideas from all your favorite far-away places and what do you get? A 'Round the World Party. Ask the birthday person to name a few foreign places of interest and build the birthday party around those special spots. Or ask what's happening in geography class this month and incorporate the sites into your theme. We've included ideas from all over the map—China, France, Canada, Germany, and Italy. So fasten your seat belts and get ready for take-off. Bon voyage!

Invitations

Here are two ideas for travel invitations.

Postcards

Old postcards (or 3×5 cards and magazine photos of foreign places)
Scissors
Glue
Felt-tip pens

If you have leftover postcards from your exciting trip to Bora Bora, use those as invitations. Your party information goes on the back, of course (ask each guest to bring a small tote bag as "baggage"). If not, make your own 3×5 cards. Cut out photos of foreign locations from magazines and trim them to fit on one side of the 3×5 card. Glue them on the cards. On the other side, divide the card in half. Write your party information on the left side and address the card on the right-hand side.

Come to my
"Round The
World" party
on August 27,
at 1:00 p.m.
R.S.V.P. to
Tommy
Warner

To Timmy Cosetti
123 El Cerro
Alamo, Calif.

Airplanes

Several 8½×11-inch sheets white
*   construction paper*
Felt-tip pens
Staples
1 large envelope per person

Fold a sheet of paper as shown at right to make a paper airplane. Unfold the paper and write your information in the area designated so that it won't show until it's unfolded again. Use the age of the birthday child as the flight number. Fill in arrival and departure times and ask each guest to bring a small tote bag as "baggage." And don't forget the destination. Then refold the airplane and staple the bottom closed. Slip into large envelopes and mail to the travelers.

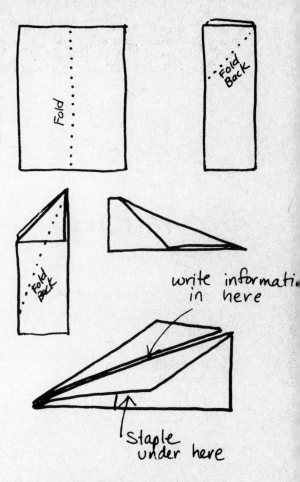

Fold

Fold Back

Fold Back

write information in here

staple under here

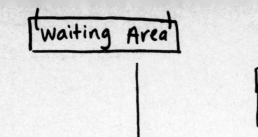

Decorations

Airport

*Several 8½ × 11-inch sheets white
    construction paper*
Felt-tip pens
String
Model planes
Large sheets of white paper for signs
Posters of planes, the sky, space
Chairs
Tape

Transform your home into an airport by hanging paper airplanes from the ceiling. (See page 127 for instructions.) If you have any airplane models, get them out of storage and hang them around the room. Mark one room of the house "Waiting Area" and put up posters of airplanes, the sky, space, and so on. In another room, arrange chairs in rows like the interior of a plane. Make a seat for the pilot and co-pilot (Mom and Dad or birthday child) with a large control panel taped to the wall.

Foreign Lands

Maps
Tape
Clear plastic sheet
*Brochures and posters from travel
    agencies*
Props from travel agencies
Foreign costume

Get out your city and state maps, unfold them, and tape them to the walls. Use one as a tablecloth (cover it with a clear plastic cover if you don't want the map decorated with dribbled food).

Visit a few travel agencies and ask for some brochures and posters of foreign lands. Hang them on your walls. If you have any toys or props that came from other lands, get them out and set them around the room or on the table. The birthday child can wear an outfit that befits a foreign country and, in the invitation, ask the guests to do the same.

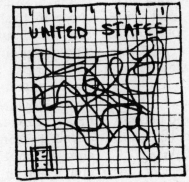

Refreshments

Runway Cake

1 cake mix, any flavor
1 11 × 15-inch piece of cardboard
Foil or doily to cover cardboard
1 can white frosting mix
1 tube red decorator frosting
1 tube green decorator frosting
Small toy airplanes
Scissors
2 straws
1 old T.V. dinner tray (or small aluminum tray) per person

Make cake according to package directions and turn into greased sheet-cake pan. When baked and cool, place on cardboard covered with doily or foil. Frost cake with white frosting. Add runway detail with decorator tubes. Add small toy airplanes to runway. Cut 1 straw into 4-inch piece and insert into

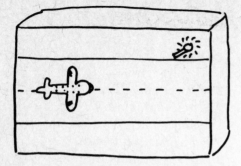

cake. Top with a dab of frosting and stick on another airplane. Stick other straw in corner of cake and top with dab of red frosting for control signal. Serve cake on old T.V. dinner trays or buy some small aluminum trays. Have kids eat in their seats. Serves 8–10.

Italian Fettucine Ice Cream

1 package brownie mix
1 12-ounce package chocolate chips
2 tablespoons light corn syrup

2 tablespoons margarine
Waxed paper
Pam or ½ teaspoon polyunsaturated oil or ½ teaspoon margarine
1 quart Italian ice cream

This is an easy ice cream and brownie dessert, topped with chocolate noodles. Prepare brownies according to package directions. Allow to cool, then cut into squares. To make chocolate fettucine, combine and heat chocolate chips, corn syrup, and margarine until melted. Lay a long strip of waxed paper on a flat surface and lightly coat with Pam, oil, or margarine. Spoon on 4 tablespoons of chocolate and top with another sheet of waxed paper, also lightly coated with Pam, oil, or margarine. Roll to ⅛-inch thick. Transfer to cookie sheet and place in refrigerator. Repeat until chocolate mixture is all rolled out. When all chocolate is pressed and cool, re-

move from refrigerator, peel off top layers of waxed paper, and allow chocolate to stand at room temperature for about 10 minutes. With a long sharp knife, cut chocolate into long strips, about ¼-inch wide. Place brownie squares in individual dishes or small plates and top with Italian ice cream that has been allowed to soften a little. Peel off strips of chocolate and loosely coil onto ice cream. Serves 4–6.

Games and Activities

Departure

Baggage claim tags
Oxygen mask
Airplane safety card
VCR and airplane movie

Greet the guests and tie baggage claim tags around their tote bags. Tie another baggage claim tag, with the guest's name on it, on each present and set aside. Have the arriving guests wait together in the "Waiting Room." When everyone has arrived, it's time for boarding. Show them into the "plane" and have each guest take a seat. The flight attendants (Mom or Dad) should go over the flight-safety rules. If you can borrow an oxygen mask from an airline (try the airport

or friends in the air travel business), give a demonstration. If you have an airplane safety card, pass it around. Ask guests to fasten their seat belts and no smoking, please. If you have a VCR or can rent one, show a few minutes from a movie that has a take-off scene, like *Airplane*.

Where Am I?

Old maps
Scissors
Glue
Tagboard
Tape
Paper and pencils

Dig out some old maps of the world or the United States or buy some inexpensive ones from the store. Select areas on the maps that give clues as to their location but do *not* give away exactly where they are. Cut out the sections and glue them onto tagboard. Hang the small area maps around the room at eye level. At game time, give each person paper and pencil and have them walk around the room and look at each map, jotting down where they think they are. Whoever gets the most right answers wins.

Pack Your Bags

1 large suitcase
Items from different countries,
*   enough for all guests*

Divide the group into two teams and have them sit in two lines. Open your suitcase and tell them you have just returned from a long trip around the world. Pass out one item to each person and tell them not to talk about it for a minute. When all guests have an item from a different country, the leader will say "Pack your bags." At that point, the last person in line hands her or his item to the next person and says the name of the item and the country it is from. (If the guest doesn't know this, he or she can ask for help.) The next person must repeat the first person's item and country, then add his or her own and pass them on,

and so on. For example, Lucy says "Koala bear from Australia," and passes it to Johnny sitting in front of her. Johnny says "Koala bear from Australia, mariachis from Mexico," and passes both items to the next person. The team that finishes first wins.

Chop, Chop, Chopsticks

1 pair of chopsticks per person
2 bowls of jelly beans, 10 in each bowl
1 empty bowl per person

This is a fast and funny game that may require a little practice first. Give everyone a pair of chopsticks and a short lesson in how to hold them (hopefully you know!). Let them practice a bit and then begin the game. Divide the group into two teams and have them sit down in two lines. Set a bowl of 10 jelly beans in front of the first ones in line. Set empty bowls in front of everyone else. When leader says "Chop, chop," the first persons in line must pick up each jellybean with a chopstick and transfer it to the first empty bowl. It is O.K. to move the empty bowl closer to the full bowl. When the second bowl is full, the next person begins to transfer the jelly beans to the third bowl, and so on. Old Chinese Proverb—The Winning Team is the First with the Full Bowl.

Favors

The little travelers can take home the airplanes and gliders. You can also give them some of the toy planes from the cake and a Golden Book about airplanes.

You can also make them some favors.

Canadian Poppers

1 cardboard tube per person, toilet roll size
Small international toys such as Chinese finger locks, Italian robots, French toilet water, and so on
1 12-inch square crepe paper per person
Ribbon
Scissors

Poppers are a friendly Canadian tradition. Fill cardboard tubes with little toys from other countries and wrap tube in crepe paper. Tie off ends with ribbon in a bow *only*, which will come off immediately when end of ribbon is pulled. Fringe ends of crepe paper with scissors. Have guests sit in a circle with poppers lying on floor in front of each one. Ask them to find one end of the ribbon on the popper to their left, then the end of the popper on the right. At the count of three, have them pull the ends of the ribbon so that all are untied together. Then they can find the surprise inside.

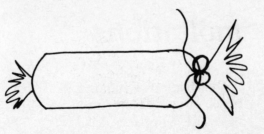

MAGIC PARTY

Magic seems to please any age group and your child will enjoy being "in on" the secrets planned for this amazing party. Just watch the cake "disappear" before your very eyes, as the tiny prestidigitators gobble it down their bottomless throats. You may want to hire a children's magician for the party but it's not necessary if you provide the entertainment we suggest on the following pages.

Invitations

This magical invitation looks like a blank piece of paper until you say the magic words.

Lemon juice
Toothpick
Pencil
White paper
Candle
1 envelope per person

Pour a small amount of lemon juice into a bowl. Dip toothpick in and write birthday information on a plain sheet of white paper. (You'll have to keep dipping the toothpick to keep the lemon juice flowing.) Let the invitation dry while you work on another. At the bottom of each sheet write instructions to hold the paper over a candle (with parental supervision) and the child will see the information appear before her or his very eyes. (You may also write with milk, but instead of using a candle to see the words, the guest must bake the paper in the oven for a few minutes.) In your invitation, ask each child to learn a magic trick to share at the party. Mail to guests.

Decorations

You can make these simple decorations "appear" out of construction paper.

Wands, Stars, and Hats

Scissors
Construction paper in various colors
Felt-tip pens
White glue
Glitter
Tape
Furry stuffed rabbit

Cut out stars, magic wands, hats, and rabbits from all colors of construction paper. Draw designs or faces and add gitter to tips of wands and to stars. Tape to walls and table. With construction paper, create a large hat by making a cylinder and a large circle and taping the large circle to the top of the cylinder. Place upside-down in the center of the table. If your child has a furry stuffed rabbit you can place in the middle, all the better. If not, make one from construction paper to peer out of the hat.

Refreshments

It's utterly amazing how quickly the refreshments disappear at a magic party. But it's certainly not a mystery!

Magical Disappearing Cake

1 package cake mix
Very small toys
Plastic lunch baggies
Scotch tape
Foil-wrapped cardboard (as large as sheet cake pan)
1 can frosting
Cut-out decorations, if desired

Bake cake according to package directions in a well-greased sheet cake pan. While cake cools, place a (very small) toy into a plastic lunch bag and fold baggie around toy; Scotch tape closed. Repeat with other toys and bags—enough for all your guests. Leave cake in pan and lightly score cake into enough pieces for guests, each piece large enough to fit toy. With a spoon scoop out a small amount of cake and insert wrapped toy. Place foil-wrapped cardboard on top of cake and flip cake over. Frost cake and decorate with stars, wands, rabbits from cut-outs, small party toys, or frosting.

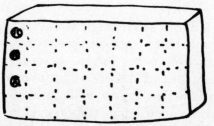

Cut cake at same dimensions you used for scoring. When you serve it, tell the children there is something magical about the cake—so eat it very carefully! You never know what might appear. Serves 8–10.

Rabbit-in-Hat Nutcups

Small paper cups
Black construction paper
Scissors
Tape
Nuts and raisins
Large marshmallows
Miniature marshmallows
Frosting tube
Toothpicks
Food coloring

Cover small cups with black construction paper. Cut out several 3½-inch black circles from construction paper to use for hat brims. Place

Games and Activities

Here are three activites to keep the little magicians under your spell.

Vanishing Gifts

As the guests arrive, surreptitiously hide the gifts that they bring. When it comes time to open presents, the birthday child will re-

alize the gifts have disappeared! Have each guest take a turn searching for a present. When the first guest finds one, have him or her bring it to the birthday person to open. Repeat until all the gifts have been found.

Mind-Reading Game

This game is prearranged with your child and it makes her or him feel very special to be "in on" the trick. Tell your guests that your child will leave the room and the guests are to choose someone who is It. When your child comes back into the room, you greet her or him with a sentence that begins with the first letter of It's name. For example, if Lucy is It, tell your child "Let us begin the mind-reading game." Since both "Lucy" and "Let us" begin with the letter "L," she or he

paper cup on circle and trace around rim; cut out inner circle. Tape brim to covered paper cup to make hat. Fill cup with nuts and raisins. Make rabbit from large marshmallows. Stick on small marshmallow ears with a dab of frosting. Paint on face with toothpick dipped in food coloring. Place rabbit on top of nuts.

should be able to guess who It is very quickly, without anyone catching on. When it's Johnny's turn to be It, say "Join our group now, oh Swami." Quiver your voice a little—it helps with the atmosphere. (Another option is for you to leave the room while your child stays.)

Magic Tricks

Have each child perform a trick for the group. Each will feel special when it is his or her turn and all the children will learn many new magic tricks to share at home. Here's one for your child:

Wear slip-on shoes for this trick. Stand facing the group with a large blanket, towel, or sheet held at waist level in front of you and hiding your feet. Show the mesmerized guests that there is nothing on the floor in front of you and wave the sheet around to show there is nothing behind the sheet. Replace the sheet in front of you and slowly step backward, gently laying the sheet on the floor as you move back. While you do this, step *out* of your shoes and cover them with the sheet. Suddenly it looks like there *is* something under that sheet—it's *lumpy!* Don't show them what it is, but touch it and prove that something is there. Then slowly lift the sheet up, walking forward and back into your shoes. Lift the sheet again and whatever it was has disappeared again! Holy Houdini!

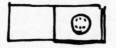

Favors

Be sure each guest takes home the special surprise that was found in the cake. You may also want to purchase some inexpensive magic tricks at the magic, toy, party, or variety store. Some good ones to look for are the Chinese finger torture, the disappearing penny, and the scarf wand.

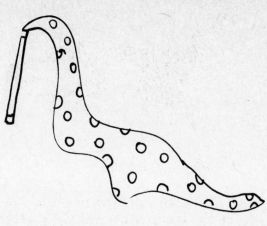

**If you enjoyed *Happy Birthday Parties!*,
you will also enjoy Penny Warner's other books:**

Super Toys: 98 easy-to-make, inexpensive toys for kids of all ages. Dozens of
fun toys and games that kids and adults can make from ordinary household
items, including dollhouses, bath toys, airplanes, kites, kaleidoscopes, jigsaw
puzzles, musical instruments, racecars, outdoor swings, and even a space
station.

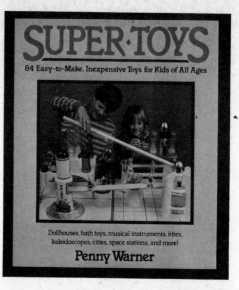

Super Snacks for Kids: over 200 fast and easy recipes that kids will enjoy eating and
that parents *and* kids will enjoy making. The emphasis is on foods that *look* fun
and have no added salt or sugar, including breakfasts, lunches, dinners, snacks,
drinks, and frozen treats.

Super Toys and *Super Snacks for Kids* are available at your local bookstore, or you can order them directly from the publisher by returning this coupon with check or money order to: St. Martin's Press, 175 Fifth Avenue, New York, N.Y. 10010, ATTN: Cash Sales. For information on credit card orders, quantity orders, and discounts, call the St. Martin's Press Special Sales Dept. toll-free at (800) 221-7945. In New York State, call (212) 674-5151.

Please send me _____ copy(ies) of
SUPER TOYS (ISBN 0-312-77658-6)
@ $8.95 per book $_____

Please send me _____ copy(ies) of
SUPER SNACKS FOR KIDS (ISBN
0-312-77636-5) @ $7.95
per book $_____

Postage and handling ($1.50 for
first copy + $.75 for each
additional) $_____

Amount enclosed $_____

Name _____

Organization _____

Address _____

City _____

State _____ Zip _____